AUTHENTIC RELATIONSHIPS:

BEING REAL IN AN ARTIFICIAL WORLD

Connect with God. Connect with Others.
Connect with Life.

Authentic Relationships: Being Real in an Artificial World
Youth Edition Student Book
© 2009 LifeWay Press®
Reprinted 2010

ISBN: 978-1-4158-6720-4
Item 005189796

Dewey Decimal Classification: 158
Subject Headings:
FRIENDSHIP \ RELATIONSHIP QUALITY \ YOUTH

Printed in the United States of America

Student Ministry Publishing
LifeWay Church Resources
One LifeWay Plaza
Nashville, TN 37234-0174

We believe that the Bible has God for its author; salvation for its end; and truth, without any mixture of error, for its matter and that all Scripture is totally true and trustworthy. The 2000 statement of *The Baptist Faith and Message* is our doctrinal guideline.

All Scripture quotations are taken from the Holman Christian Standard Bible®, copyright © 1999, 2000, 2002, 2003 by Holman Bible Publishers. Used by permission.

CONTENTS

EXPERIENCE

Combine teaching that engages a large-group with dynamic small-group experiences and discussions and you end up grappling with reality and experiencing real life change. Throughout 13 sessions, small groups will find power in just being together and connecting.

 Get Ready

To get the most from this experience, spend some time with God each day leading up to your group session. Wrap your brain around the short Bible passages, listen to God, and jot down thoughts and insights.

 **So What?**

The master teacher will lead the entire group in understanding what God has to say on the topic. Content is deep, but engaging. Follow along, jot notes, and respond to questions in your book.

 LifePoint

Your large-group leader will welcome everyone. You'll hear the "LifePoint" or big idea for the session, and then divide into small groups.

 Do What?

All study should direct us toward action and life change. It's easier and more helpful to discuss application in small groups. The goal is to be real with each other in order to connect with God and each other. Find power in the support and prayers of other students.

 Say What?

Enjoy fun, interactive experiences and discussions in your small group. Discuss the "Random Question of the Week" and join activities or discussions that lead into the session topic.

 now What?

To see real power in your life, you don't want to leave the session and just go on with life as normal. The "Now What?" assignments help you continue your journey and give you an opportunity to go deeper with God.

YOUTH *AT A GLANCE*

Get Ready

Daily time with God
& your journal

LifePoint

Large Group:
welcome & theme

Say What?

Small Group:
fun & interaction

So What?

Large Group:
teaching & discovery
(master teacher)

Do What?

Small Group:
getting real
& connecting

Now What?

Continue your journey . . .

GROUP COVENANT

It is important that your group covenant together, agreeing to live out important group values. Once these values are agreed upon, your group will be on its way to experiencing true Christian community. It's very important that your group discuss these values—preferably as you begin this study. The first session would be most appropriate. (Check the rules to which each member of your group agrees.)

☐ Priority: While you are in this course of study, you give the group meetings priority.

☐ Participation: Everyone is encouraged to participate and no one dominates.

☐ Respect: Everyone is given the right to his or her own opinion, and all questions are encouraged and respected.

☐ Confidentiality: Anything that is said in the meeting is never repeated outside the meeting without permission. Note: Church staff may be required by law to report illegal activities.

☐ Life Change: We will regularly assess our own progress in applying "LifePoints" and encourage one another in our pursuit of becoming more like Christ.

☐ Care and Support: Permission is given to call upon each other at any time, especially in times of crisis. The group will provide care for every member.

☐ Accountability: We agree to let the members of the group hold us accountable to the commitments we make in whatever loving ways we decide upon. Giving unsolicited advice is not permitted.

☐ Empty Chair: The group is open to welcoming new people at every meeting.

☐ Mission: We agree as a group to reach out and invite others to join us.

☐ Ministry: We will encourage one another to volunteer and serve in a ministry and to support missions by giving financially and/or personally serving.

1

BEING A REAL FRIEND

 Get Ready

Read one of these short Bible passages each day, and spend a few minutes of focused time with God. Be sure to jot down any insights you receive.

MONDAY **Read John 15:9.**
Who is someone you know for sure loves you? How does this person show his or her love to you? How do you know God loves you? What are some specific ways He has shown His love to you? How do you believe you "remain in His love"?

TUESDAY **Read John 15:10.**
How are *love* and *obedience* related to each other? How does your obedience to God's commands help you remain in His love? How does your obedience to God's commands show that you love Him?

WEDNESDAY **Read John 15:11.**
When was the last time you felt like you had God's complete joy in you? Why does lovingly obeying God bring joy? How can this joy overflow into your friendships?

THURSDAY

Read John 15:12-13.

How has a friend sacrificed for you? How have you sacrificed for a friend? Why is sacrifice part of a loving friendship?

FRIDAY

Read John 15:15.

Who is a special friend to you? How would you describe your relationship with this person? Do you think of yourself as one of Jesus' friends? Through your friendship with Jesus, what has He taught you about our Father?

SATURDAY

Read John 15:16.

How do you know that Jesus chose you? Why did He choose you? What kind of "fruit" does He want you to produce? What promise does Jesus make? Does this mean that God will give you anything you ask for?

SUNDAY

Read John 15:16-17.

Is there someone who is hard for you to love? What did Jesus command in these verses? How can you show others that you love them?

 LifePoint

Through His love and sacrifice, Jesus modeled what it means to be a real friend.

SMALL-GROUP TIME:

Divide into groups of four to eight, preferably in a circle configuration. You will have a small-group leader for "Say What?"

 # Say What? (15 minutes)

Random Question of the Week:

What is one of the funniest or silliest things you've ever done with one of your best friends?

Group Experience: Friendship

Answer the following questions and be prepared to share your responses.

1. What do you believe it takes to be a real friend?
   - ☐ money
   - ☐ loyalty
   - ☐ willingness to share food
   - ☐ honesty
   - ☐ the ability to put others first
   - ☐ good looks
   - ☐ a winning personality
   - ☐ sense of humor
   - ☐ good dental hygiene
   - ☐ courage
   - ☐ other: _____

2. How do you choose your friends? When was the last time you made a new friend?

3. What is one of the greatest sacrifices a friend has made for you? How about you for a friend? Why do friends make sacrifices for each other?

LARGE-GROUP
TIME:
Turn to face the
front for this
teaching time.
Follow along and
take notes in your
student book.

 # So What? (30 minutes)

Real Friendships

1. How would you define a "real friend"?

2. How did Jesus model real friendship?

3. How can we develop friendships that are real?

Learning from the Bible

John 15:9-17

[9] *"As the Father has loved Me, I have also loved you. Remain in My love. [10] If you keep My commands you will remain in My love, just as I have kept My Father's commands and remain in His love.*

[11] *"I have spoken these things to you so that My joy may be in you and your joy may be complete. [12] This is My command: love one another as I have loved you. [13] No one has greater love than this, that someone would lay down his life for his friends. [14] You are My friends if you do what I command you. [15] I do not call you slaves anymore, because a slave doesn't know what his master is doing. I have called you friends, because I have made known to you everything I have heard from My Father. [16] You did not choose Me, but I chose you. I appointed you that you should go out and produce fruit and that your fruit should remain, so that whatever you ask the Father in My name, He will give you. [17] This is what I command you: love one another."*

Not a Typical Friendship

4. How is friendship with Jesus different than friendship with a peer?

Qualities of a Real Friendship

5. Why is it vital for friends to reveal their true thoughts and wishes?

6. Why do friends need to respect each others' wishes?

7. What kinds of sacrifices might friends have to make for each other?

8. Why is it important for friends to encourage each other to develop and to use their talents?

SMALL-GROUP
TIME:
Small-group
leaders will direct
your discussions.
Everyone will gain
more if you are
open and honest
in responding to
the questions.

Do What? (15 minutes)

Making It Personal

1. Of the things Jesus talked about in this passage, which one is most important to you in a friendship? Explain your answer.
   - ☐ Friends share their true thoughts and feelings to each other.
   - ☐ Friends respect each other's wishes.
   - ☐ Friends sacrifice for each other.
   - ☐ Friends encourage each other to develop and use their talents.

2. Think about your closest friends. Mark on the following scales with a circle, ranking yourself between 1 and 10 (with 1 being never and 10 being always) in how you believe you do each action for your friends. Mark on the same scales with a square, ranking your friends on how they do these actions for you.

I share my true thoughts and feelings to my friends.

1   2   3   4   5   6   7   8   9   10

My friends share their true thoughts and feelings to me.

I respect my friends' wishes.

1   2   3   4   5   6   7   8   9   10

My friends respect my wishes.

I sacrifice for my friends.

1   2   3   4   5   6   7   8   9   10

My friends sacrifice for me.

I encourage my friends to develop and use their talents.

1   2   3   4   5   6   7   8   9   10

My friends encourage me to develop and use my talents.

3. To be a better friend to others, which of the following do you most need to work on? Explain your answer.
   ☐ sharing my true thoughts and feelings
   ☐ respecting the desires of others
   ☐ sacrificing for others
   ☐ encouraging my friends to develop and use their talents

 LifePoint Review

Through His love and sacrifice, Jesus modeled what it means to be a real friend.

"Do" Points

These "Do" points will help you begin to experience this week's "LifePoint." Be open and honest as you discuss the action points within your small group.

1. <u>Set aside at least three hours this coming week to focus on building friendships.</u> This time could be used to call or text friends just to see how they are doing. It could be used for taking a friend out for a special treat or for helping a friend with a task he or she has been assigned. Or it could be for just hanging out together, enjoying an activity that is fun for both of you.

2. <u>Share something new about yourself with a friend and discover something new about him or her.</u> Find some time to just sit and visit with one of your friends. Choose someone you trust and whom you want to know better. Make sure there is nothing to distract you like cell phones, the Internet, or television. Share two or three significant things about yourself that you think your friend does not already know about you. Ask him or her to do the same. Discuss how it feels to share so openly with each other.

3. <u>Identify at least two special talents a specific friend has and encourage him or her in at least one of them.</u> Encouraging a friend can mean anything from complimenting how you've seen him or her use a talent, to attending an event (concert, game, worship service, class, and so forth) during which your friend is using that talent and giving positive feedback about what you experience.

Prayer Connection:

This is the time for developing and expressing concern for each other. Thank God for the friendship of Jesus and ask Him to make you an authentic friend to others.

Share prayer needs and requests with the group, especially those related to hearing from and responding to God. Your group facilitator will close your time in prayer.

Prayer Needs:

Remember your
"Get Ready" daily
Bible readings
and questions at
the beginning of
session 2.

 now What?

There is an old saying, "To have a friend you've got to be one." The idea behind this saying is that if we are self-focused, concerned about what we do or do not have in terms of friendship, then we won't be considering the acts of friendship that others need. As a result, they'll have no reason to be our friend. Deepen your understanding of who God is and His desire for you to have and to be a real friend, and continue the journey you've begun today by choosing one of the following assignments to complete this week:

Option #1
Give one of your friends a call and express your desire to really make a difference in his or her life. Ask if there is something you can do to help him or her out this week. Ensure that your friend understands you are willing to make some kind of sacrifice on his or her behalf. Make sure you follow through! Thank your friend for this opportunity to serve him or her.

Option #2
Get out of your comfort zone this week by looking outside your circle of friends. Consider someone new in your neighborhood, school, or church who might need a friend. Make an effort to contact this person and spend time with him or her. Introduce this person to your other friends. Include this person the next time you and your friends get together. In this new friendship, apply the principles you learned in this session: Be open. Respect his or her wishes. Make sacrifices for him or her. Encourage him or her to develop and use their talents for God.

Bible Reference Notes

Use these notes to gain further understanding of the text as you study on your own.

John 15:10 *If you keep my commands.* Which commands? The commands to love! Jesus had just referred to His "new command" that they love one another (John 13:34; 15:12). The other gospels record that Jesus said the two greatest commandments are to love God with all our hearts, minds, and souls, and to love our neighbor as ourselves (Matt. 22:34-40; Mark 12:28-34; Luke 10:25-28).

John 15:11 *your joy may be complete.* Joy that is focused on one's own well-being alone is not complete. Only joy that sees our connection with God and with all God's creatures is complete because it is joy that does not require the other's sadness.

John 15:13 *No one has greater love than this.* The ultimate example of this was Jesus' own sacrifice on the cross. Some have said this is a narrower concept than the concept that Christ died for all. But the words of verse 14, "You are My friends if you do what I command you" mean that the choice lies with us. All have the opportunity to be Christ's friends.

John 15:15 *slaves . . . friends.* A relationship of servitude is based on power. A relationship of friendship is based on love. Jesus, in His love, has made His followers privy to information normally only shared among colleagues, not between a master and his servants. Still, this friendship is not one of equals, for it is predicated upon obedience on the part of the disciples.

John 15:16 *You did not choose Me, but I chose you.* Some have interpreted this to mean that people have no choice in becoming a Christian—Christ chooses us. However, this passage may be seen as nothing more than historical reality about the first disciples—Jesus went out looking for them, as the gospels make evident (Matt. 4:18-22).

produce fruit and that your fruit should remain. Jesus is promising that what they accomplish through Him won't be transitory; it will be as eternal as God's kingdom.

notes

Session

2

SHOWING REAL LOYALTY

 Get Ready

Read one of these short Bible passages each day, and spend a few minutes of focused time with God. Be sure to jot down any insights you receive.

MONDAY

Read Ruth 1:1-10.
Sometimes authentic friendships are greatly tested by life circumstances. In which of your friendships has this type of difficulty occurred?

TUESDAY

Read Ruth 1:11-13.
What side benefits do you typically expect from your friendships? What benefit is there in someone being a friend with you?

WEDNESDAY

Read Ruth 1:14-17.
Why is it challenging to remain friends with someone who is going through a difficult time?

THURSDAY

Read Ruth 1:16.
How willing are you to stay committed to your friends? What might get in the way of your commitment to your friends?

FRIDAY

Read Ruth 1:16.

At some point in Naomi and Ruth's relationship, Ruth discovered Naomi's God. Do your friends know about your relationship with God? How important is it to you to talk about your faith in God with your friends?

SATURDAY

Read Ruth 1:16-17.

Reflect on what has separated you from friends in the past. In thinking back, should you have let this separate you? Is there hope that this friendship can be restored?

SUNDAY

Read Ruth 1:18.

Reflect on how determined you are to demonstrate loyalty to your friends. What personal sacrifices might have to be made for you to stay loyal to your friends? What specific ways can you show your loyalty?

 # LifePoint

Loyalty is a key ingredient in authentic, committed relationships.

SMALL-GROUP TIME:

Divide into groups of four to eight, preferably in a circle configuration. You will have a small-group leader for "Say What?"

 # Say What? (15 minutes)

Random Question of the Week:

What is your favorite flavor of ice cream?

Group Experience: Loyalty

Answer the following questions and be prepared to share your responses.

1. Fill in the blank: _____ is my most loyal friend. List three reasons why you have selected this friend.
   1.
   2.
   3.

2. Which of your friends do you believe would classify you as his or her most loyal friend? _____ List three reasons why you believe he or she would say this about you.
   1.
   2.
   3.

3. One quality that tops the list in survey after survey of what people appreciate most about their friends is loyalty. Take the following test to determine how loyal you are by ranking yourself on a scale of 1 to 10, with 1 being never and 10 being always.

I am only friends with people as long as it benefits me.

1   2   3   4   5   6   7   8   9   10

I am loyal to some of my friends but not to others.

1   2   3   4   5   6   7   8   9   10

I believe loyalty in friendship is overrated.

1   2   3   4   5   6   7   8   9   10

If a friend's life gets too messy, I am out of there!

1   2   3   4   5   6   7   8   9   10

I believe that loyalty is an essential requirement to be a good friend.

1   2   3   4   5   6   7   8   9   10

My friends can always count on me.

1   2   3   4   5   6   7   8   9   10

I go through friends like I go through socks!

1   2   3   4   5   6   7   8   9   10

I can recall specific examples of times when I have demonstrated loyalty to my friends.

1   2   3   4   5   6   7   8   9   10

What do your test results indicate about how loyal of a friend you are?

LARGE-GROUP TIME:
Turn to face the front for this teaching time. Follow along and take notes in your student book.

 # So What? (30 minutes)

Real Loyalty

1. How would you define the word *loyalty?*

2. What does *loyalty* between friends look like?

3. In what context was the Book of Ruth written, and why does it serve as a good example of authentic friendship?

Learning from the Bible

Ruth 1:1-18

¹ During the time of the judges, there was a famine in the land. A man left Bethlehem in Judah with his wife and two sons to live in the land of Moab for a while. ² The man's name was Elimelech, and his wife's name was Naomi. The names of his two sons were Mahlon and Chilion. They were Ephrathites from Bethlehem in Judah. They entered the land of Moab and settled there. ³ Naomi's husband Elimelech died, and she was left with her two sons. ⁴ Her sons took Moabite women as their wives: one was named Orpah and the second was named Ruth. After they lived in Moab about 10 years, ⁵ both Mahlon and Chilion also died, and Naomi was left without her two children and without her husband.

*⁶ She and her daughters-in-law prepared to leave the land of Moab, because she had heard in Moab that the L*ORD* had paid attention to His people's need by providing* them food. [7] She left the place where she had been living, accompanied by her two daughters-in-law, and traveled along the road leading back to the land of Judah.

[8] She said to them, "Each of you go back to your mother's home. May the LORD show faithful love to you as you have shown to the dead and to me. [9] May the LORD enable each of you to find security in the house of your new husband." She kissed them, and they wept loudly.

[10] "No," they said to her. "We will go with you to your people."

[11] But Naomi replied, "Return home, my daughters. Why do you want to go with me? Am I able to have any more sons who could become your husbands? [12] Return home, my daughters. Go on, for I am too old to have another husband. Even if I thought there was still hope for me to have a husband tonight and to bear sons, [13] would you be willing to wait for them to grow up? Would you restrain yourselves from remarrying? No, my daughters, my life is much too bitter for you to share, because the LORD's hand has turned against me." [14] Again they wept loudly, and Orpah kissed her mother-in-law, but Ruth clung to her. [15] Naomi said, "Look, your sister-in-law has gone back to her people and to her god. Follow your sister-in-law."

[16] But Ruth replied,

> Do not persuade me to leave you
> or go back and not follow you.
> For wherever you go, I will go,
> and wherever you live, I will live;
> your people will be my people,
> and your God will be my God.
> [17] Where you die, I will die,
> and there I will be buried.
> May the LORD do this to me,
> and even more,
> if anything but death separates you and me.

[18] When Naomi saw that Ruth was determined to go with her, she stopped trying to persuade her.

Loyalty Stronger Than Blood Ties

4. Why do family members typically display loyalty for each other?

5. How did Jesus also demonstrate loyalty for those outside of His biological family?

Loyalty Stronger Than Cultural Ties

6. What other Old Testament books questioned the ethnocentric idea that God was only interested in Israel and wanted foreigners to be shunned?

7. Because of her loyalty, to whom did Ruth end up being an ancestor?

Loyalty Stronger Than Self-fulfillment

8. Why did Naomi encourage Ruth and Orpah to go back home?

9. How did Ruth demonstrate that her loyalty to Naomi was greater than her own need for self-fulfillment?

10. What modern situation might make a person feel like they are in the same situation as Ruth and Naomi were in?

SMALL-GROUP TIME: Small-group leaders will direct your discussions. Everyone will gain more if you are open and honest in responding to the questions.

 Do What? (15 minutes)

Making It Personal

1. Assuming you did not know how the story ended, what would you have done had you been in Ruth's shoes?

☐ I would have been out of there—I don't deal well with poverty!

☐ I would have headed home—I'm still my parents' child at heart!

☐ I would have been like Orpah—offered to go with Naomi, but relieved to have an out.

☐ I would have gone with Naomi—I'm the adventurous type!

☐ I would have gone with Naomi—going home is not an attractive option in my case.

☐ I would have gone with Naomi—I'm as loyal as the family dog!

☐ Other: _____

2. Once you had decided to go with Naomi, what would have been the main focus of your hope for the future?

☐ Finding someone who could come along and save us!

☐ Hey, with a real friend by your side you can face anything!

☐ I would have figured we needed a miracle of God.

☐ I'm not sure I would have had any hope.

☐ Other: _____

3. What would you say is the biggest reward for showing loyalty like Ruth did?

☐ God's rewards for such behavior—like when He gave Ruth and Boaz to each other

☐ The quality of the friendship that comes out of it

☐ If you are loyal to others, others will be loyal to you when you need it.

☐ Just knowing you did the right thing is reward enough.

☐ Other: _____

LifePoint Review

Loyalty is a key ingredient in authentic, committed relationships.

"Do" Points

These "Do" points will help you begin to experience this week's "LifePoint." Be open and honest as you discuss the action points within your small group.

1. <u>Make a list of times when another person stuck by you when it wasn't necessarily to his or her advantage.</u> By focusing on times when others stood by you, you will learn more about what it means to be truly loyal to others. Take time this week to

thank this person for his or her demonstration of loyalty. Look for opportunities to display the same loyalty to this person—even if it is not to your advantage.

2. <u>Write out a vow of loyalty to someone with whom you are in a relationship.</u> Being loyal means you can be trusted with important information. Reliability and respect are earned by proving that you are a trustworthy friend. Standing by a friend during a time when others forsake him or her will prove that you are a true friend. Using a format similar to Ruth's in Ruth 1:1-18, write and send a letter to a friend expressing your willingness to display this same kind of loyalty in your relationship with him or her.

3. <u>Make a commitment to thank God daily for His faithfulness.</u> When you have a personal relationship with God, He sticks with you no matter what. He will never give up on you. He proved the level of His faithfulness toward you by sending His Son to die on the cross for you. Remembering the faithful loyalty of God on a daily basis will remind you of the same loyalty you should extend to those with whom you have a personal relationship. Every day, for the next week, thank God for His devotion to you.

Prayer Connection:

This is the time for developing and expressing concern for each other. Finish this sentence: Right now I need a "Ruth" to stand by me in the midst of _____. Pray for God's guidance and strength in responding to whatever needs are mentioned. Close by thanking God for bringing you together as a group and by asking Him to help you be loyal in your relationships.

Share prayer needs and requests with the group, especially those related to hearing from and responding to God. Your group facilitator will close your time in prayer.

Prayer Needs:

Remember your "Get Ready" daily Bible readings and questions at the beginning of session 3.

now What?

Many of us have been where Ruth and Naomi were in this story. Someone we loved died, our families had financial problems, and the future seemed to hold nothing but fear. Others have never faced such a situation, but know what it is like to fear difficult life circumstances. Who will still be with us if such a thing happens? As we have pointed out, to have such loyal relationships we need to be loyal ourselves. Here are some suggestions for building loyal relationships.

Option #1

Take time this week to read the rest of Ruth's story. On a piece of paper or in your personal journal, record examples of circumstances in which Ruth continued to demonstrate loyalty toward others. Record examples of circumstances in which others demonstrated loyalty toward Ruth. After you have finished reading the Book of Ruth, consider what else you have discovered about what it means to be loyal to others. Look for opportunities to put what you have learned into action.

Option #2

The kind of loyalty presented in this study today should extend beyond your friendships to your family members. It's important for the people you live with to know they can count on you, too. In the next week, watch for specific ways you can demonstrate loyalty to every member of your family.

Bible Reference notes

Use these notes to gain further understanding of the text as you study on your own.

Ruth 1:1

During the time of the judges. This was from 1375 B.C. to about 1075 B.C. Apparently, at the time of this writing it was no longer the case that the judges ruled, so it was probably written in the early years of the kingships. Stories like this would have been passed along carefully by word of mouth. Such story-telling was an art form in the ancient Near East. It is significant that Ruth is placed right after Judges in the Bible. It provides an interesting contrast: Judges chronicled how Israel had difficulty showing loyalty to God, while Ruth tells of a foreign woman whose loyalty was exemplary.

there was a famine in the land. Such a famine was also the cause of the migration of Jacob's family to Egypt (Gen. 42-47).

a man left Bethlehem. This foreshadows one of the central results of this story: Ruth and Boaz were great-grandparents of David (Ruth 4:21-22) and Bethlehem was called the City of David. For Christians, it also reminds us that these were ancestors of Jesus Christ, also born in Bethlehem.

Ruth 1:2

Ephrathites. First Chronicles 2:19-20,50 suggests that Bethlehem was founded by the descendants of a woman named Ephrath, the wife of Caleb.

Ruth 1:4

Her sons took Moabite women. Moab was a traditional enemy of Israel (Num. 22 and 25). Taking foreign wives was a highly controversial activity for an Israelite. In Deuteronomy 7:1-4 God warned the Israelites not to take foreign wives. Although Moab is not listed there specifically, it is mentioned in 1 Kings 11:1-4, where King Solomon's marriage to foreign women is referred to as a violation of this ban on foreign marriages. In addition, Deuteronomy 23:3 bans Moabites and their descendants down to the tenth generation from entering "the LORD's assembly." And yet King David was a third generation descendant of a Moabite woman (Ruth 4:21-22)! While there is a mystery in these conflicting reports, it seems evident that God chose this foreign woman to eventually bring to the world the Savior who broke down the dividing walls between Jews and Gentiles (Eph. 2:11-17).

Ruth 1:5

Naomi was left without her two children and without her husband. Women in these times were almost totally dependent on men economically. They could not get a job that paid much. This meant that the plight of these women was desperate indeed.

Ruth 1:8

Each of you go back to your mother's home. Generally, women were advised to go back to their "father's house" (Gen. 38:11; Lev. 22:13). Why is the phrase different here? Perhaps their fathers were dead. Some commentators have suggested that the writer of Ruth was one with a peculiar empathy for the plight and value of women, and this phrase that is unusual for its time might reflect that.

Ruth 1:10

We will go with you to your people. This first offer would have been the polite thing to do in this culture. Only if they persisted after further insistence that they leave would this offer to stay with Naomi be thought of as what they really wanted to do. In modern culture, the closest comparison might be when one person at the table in a restaurant offers to pick up the check and the other says, "No, you don't have to do that." Persistence differentiates sincerity from politeness.

Ruth 1:11

any more sons. According to the teaching of Deuteronomy 25:5-6, the brother of a man who died without a son would be obligated to marry his widow and raise up a son for him.

Ruth 1:13

the LORD's hand has turned against me. It was assumed in those days that suffering was the result of God's judgment on a person—an assumption that was questioned by the Book of Job. Naomi saw her circumstances as worse than for Ruth and Orpah because they were young enough to get remarried, while she had little hope for such happening.

Ruth 1:16

Do not persuade me to leave you. This well-known saying is often used as part of weddings, but in the original context it is a vow of loyalty from one woman to another.

Session
3

·DEVELOPING REAL·INTIMACY

 Get Ready

Read one of these short Bible passages each day, and spend a few minutes of focused time with God. Be sure to jot down any insights you receive.

MONDAY

Read 1 Samuel 18:1-3.

How can you tell that you have "clicked" with someone? Whom do you love as much as yourself? How do you express your love to that person?

TUESDAY

Read 1 Samuel 18:4-5.

How generous are you in giving to your friends? What, if anything, holds you back from giving more generously to them? Why does sacrificial giving create real intimacy among friends?

WEDNESDAY

Read Samuel 18:6-9.

Why is jealousy destructive to friendships? What is typically the cause of jealousy? How is jealousy interfering with your friendships right now?

THURSDAY

Read Proverbs 17:17.

In what ways have you become closer to a friend with whom you have shared adversity? Who is a friend who has loved you no matter what?

FRIDAY **Read Proverbs 18:24.**

Do your current friendships indicate you are focused more on developing one or two close friends or on a big network of acquaintances? While you do need to be friendly to everyone, why is it important for you to have a close-knit group of friends?

SATURDAY **Read Proverbs 27:5.**

Do you hide who you truly are from your friends or do you feel the freedom to openly express yourself? Why is it difficult to handle a "rebuke" from a friend?

SUNDAY **Read Ecclesiastes 4:9-12.**

Why do we need to be in an intimate relationship with others? How have you and your friends supported each other when one of you have fallen or struggled in some way? How does intimate friendship make us stronger?

 LifePoint

True intimacy is available among friends who can openly trust each other and who are willing to make sacrifices for each other.

SMALL-GROUP TIME:

Divide into groups of four to eight, preferably in a circle configuration. You will have a small-group leader for "Say What?"

Say What? (15 minutes)

Random Question of the Week:

If you were blindfolded, could you tell the difference between regular and diet cola just by holding the bottles or cans in your hands?

Group Experience: Intimacy

Answer the following questions and be prepared to share your responses.

1. As a child, what rituals or actions do you remember doing to symbolize a friendship?
   - ☐ Cutting fingers to become "blood brothers/sisters"
   - ☐ Exchanging clothes or jewelry
   - ☐ Developing a special handshake
   - ☐ Developing a special, exclusive "club"
   - ☐ Developing your own special "language"
   - ☐ Other: _____

2. Who is your closest friend? What makes this friendship so special?

3. What could you give to a friend today to symbolize your friendship with him or her?

4. What are key ingredients to developing real intimacy in friendships? (Check any of the following that you believe apply.) Be prepared to explain why you marked each statement.
   - ☐ There's not much you can do—it's mostly chemistry.
   - ☐ Work at it—such friendships don't happen overnight.
   - ☐ Be open—you have to share who you are.
   - ☐ Trust—you can't feel as if you have to watch your back.
   - ☐ Be self-giving instead of self-focused—there's no room for big egos in friendship.
   - ☐ Other: _____

LARGE-GROUP TIME:

Turn to face the front for this teaching time. Follow along and take notes in your student book.

 # So What? (30 minutes)

True Intimacy

1. How would you define true intimacy?

2. Why is it important to understand that intimacy is different from sexual desire?

3. How has the level of intimacy between Jonathan and David been misunderstood? Why is this common today?

4. What other biblical men are mentioned who had close friendships? Can you think of any others?

Learning from the Bible

1 Samuel 18:1-9

[1] When David had finished speaking with Saul, Jonathan committed himself to David, and loved him as much as he loved himself. [2] Saul kept David with him from that day on and did not let him return to his father's house.

[3] Jonathan made a covenant with David because he loved him as much as himself.
[4] Then Jonathan removed the robe he was wearing and gave it to David, along with his military tunic, his sword, his bow, and his belt.

[5] David marched out with the army, and was successful in everything Saul sent him to do. Saul put him in command of the soldiers, which pleased all the people and Saul's servants as well.

[6] As David was returning from killing the Philistine, the women came out from all the cities of Israel to meet King Saul, singing and dancing with tambourines, with shouts of joy, and with three-stringed instruments. [7] As they celebrated, the women sang:

Saul has killed his thousands,
but David his tens of thousands."

⁸ Saul was furious and resented this song. "They credited tens of thousands to David,"
he complained, "but they only credited me with thousands. What more can he have but
the kingdom?" ⁹ So Saul watched David jealously from that day forward.

Jonathan's Symbolic Gestures

5. What is the significance of Jonathan giving David his robe?

6. Why is such openness an essential part of developing an intimate relationship with someone else?

7. What was the significance of Jonathan's giving David his armor?

8. Why did Jonathan trust David?

9. Why do we have to choose to trust others in order to develop an intimate relationship with them?

10. What will help us learn to trust others?

Jonathan Showed He Could Be Trusted

11. How did Jonathan prove his trustworthiness to David?

SMALL-GROUP TIME:

Small-group leaders will direct your discussions. Everyone will gain more if you are open and honest in responding to the questions.

 **Do What?** (15 minutes)

Making It Personal

1. When do you remember jealousy threatening or destroying a friendship you had, as it did between David and Saul? If this is still an issue, what steps can you take to restore intimacy in this friendship?

2. If you were to give a friend something right now, something that would symbolize who you are, what might you give?

3. What is the closest you have come to having a friendship like Jonathan and David had?

4. What do you need to do personally to develop real intimacy in your friendships? (Check any of the following that you believe apply.) Be prepared to explain why you marked each statement.
   - ☐ Take time to work on being a friend.
   - ☐ Be more open—share more about who I really am.
   - ☐ Learn to trust again—I've been burned.
   - ☐ Get my focus off myself.
   - ☐ Nothing—I'm doing all I can.
   - ☐ Other: _____

# LifePoint Review

True intimacy is available among friends who can openly trust each other and who are willing to make sacrifices for each other.

"Do" Points

These "Do" points will help you begin to experience this week's "LifePoint." Be open and honest as you discuss the action points within your small group.

3

1. <u>Reveal at least one thing about yourself that you don't normally reveal.</u> On a sheet of paper, record five things about yourself that you don't normally reveal to others. You may want to start with something less threatening, then progress from there. Choose one thing on this list and share it with either a friend or a member of your small group with whom you have already established an intimate relationship.

2. <u>Choose something you would normally do yourself and entrust it to a friend.</u> This could be a responsibility you have at home or it could be a task for school, a school club or an after-school job. Your friends need to know that you need them. They need to know that you trust them to do things that are important to you, just as David trusted Jonathan with his life. Ask your friends if you can return the favor. After you have done these things, meet together and discuss what it felt like to trust these responsibilities to each other.

3. <u>Give a gift to a friend that says something about yourself.</u> Think about your closest friends. Choose one special friend with whom you have already established trust and openness. Give a gift to him or her that shows your values, your feelings, or your interests. Explain to this friend the meaning behind the gift and why you chose to give it. Make sure the gift is something that will also be special to your friend.

Prayer Connection:

This is the time for developing and expressing concern for each other. Thank God for the example He provided through the friendship of David and Jonathan. Ask God to help you find the same kind of intimacy in your own friendships.

Share prayer needs and requests with the group, especially those related to hearing from and responding to God. Your group facilitator will close your time in prayer.

Prayer Needs:

Remember your "Get Ready" daily Bible readings and questions at the beginning of session 4.

Now What?

Those of us who have not recently had intimate friendships might look at the story of David and Jonathan with a bit of envy and even despair. We might think we could never develop such a friendship. Or we might feel that this friendship may become just another of our surrogate friendships, like we have with characters on TV shows. But, that's not the way it has to be. We can build intimate friendships if we do it one step at a time. Here are some suggestions to help you get started:

3

Option #1

One of the greatest acts of intimacy you will share with friends is to pray for each other. Purchase or create a simple prayer journal for you and your circle of friends. Create an image on the front of this journal that represents each unique member of this prayer group. Meet once a week to share prayer requests and concerns with each other. Close this time of intimate sharing by praying out loud for each other. To ensure that each person feels safe in openly speaking what is on his or her heart, make a commitment to each other that you will not talk about this information anywhere outside of this prayer time.

Option #2

You can take your current friendships to a whole new level of intimacy by being willing to be open and honest with each other. Discuss this with your closest friends. Are you able to be open and honest with each other? Do you trust each other to guard the things you share in confidence? Can you honestly say that you defend each other and put each other's needs first? Using a Bible concordance or a Web site like *www.biblegateway.com*, find a time for you and your closest friends to study passages of Scripture or Bible stories about friendship. Do your best to ensure that everyone feels comfortable discussing the spiritual truths and principles you discover about friendship.

Bible Reference Notes

Use these notes to gain further understanding of the text as you study on your own.

1 Samuel 18:1   *When David had finished speaking with Saul.* They had been talking about David's slaying of the Philistine giant, Goliath (1 Sam. 17:1-58).

he loved him as much as he loved himself. Jonathan related to David naturally in the way we are commanded to love others (Lev. 19:18; Matt. 22:34-40; Mark 12:28-34; Luke 10:25-28).

1 Samuel 18:3   *made a covenant.* This was a formal, legally binding type of agreement. A covenant was sealed with some kind of sign. The rainbow was the sign of the covenant God made with Noah. Circumcision was a sign of the covenant the people of Israel made with God. The gifts Jonathan gave were a seal of this covenant of friendship.

1 Samuel 18:4   *the robe he was wearing.* Clothing in this day indicated your status. This robe would have marked his identity as royalty.

his military tunic . . . his belt. By giving his armor to David, it showed that Jonathan trusted him and was willing to be vulnerable to him.

1 Samuel 18:6   *the women came out.* While in many respects women didn't have much value in these times, their praises and songs after a military victory would have been important to the male egos of combatants and generals.

1 Samuel 18:8   *What more can he have but the kingdom?* Saul knew that he had displeased God earlier by his disobedience and that God had decided to turn the kingdom over to another (1 Sam. 15:1-16:14). No doubt he saw that this was going to happen through David, and he sought to avoid this judgment by his acts of violence and jealousy (1 Sam. 18:10-16).

SHOWING REAL TRUST

 ## Get Ready

Read one of these short Bible passages each day, and spend a few minutes of focused time with God. Be sure to jot down any insights you receive.

MONDAY

Read Matthew 1:18-19.

What event occurred that Joseph initially perceived to be a violation of trust? What relationship have you considered ending because of a breach of trust? Why did you consider ending this relationship?

TUESDAY

Read Matthew 1:20-21.

What new information did God give to Joseph about Mary's pregnancy? What fear do you need to overcome in order to reach out to someone who has hurt you? Have you considered if you have all the facts about the situation through which this offense occurred?

WEDNESDAY

Read Matthew 1:22-23.

Reflect on how God has been faithful to His promises in your life. How does His faithfulness to you in the past help you to trust Him in the future?

THURSDAY

Read Matthew 1:23-24.

How has God been present with you in this past week? How does His presence help you to trust others?

FRIDAY

Read Matthew 1:24-25.

God challenged Joseph to trust Him. Joseph demonstrated his trust in God through obedience. How is God challenging you to trust Him right now? How can you obediently demonstrate your trust in Him?

Read Psalm 56:1-4.

In what situation are you currently being challenged to demonstrate trust? How are you presently showing your trust in God through your actions?

Read Psalm 56:1-4.

How can trusting God help you trust others?

 # LifePoiNt

Trust is one of the fundamental elements of a good relationship.

Say What? (15 minutes)

Random Question of the Week:
How long can you hold your breath? Prove it.

Group Experience: Trust
Answer the following questions and be prepared to share your responses.

1. Of all your personal relationships, whom do you trust the most? Why do you trust this person? How do your actions prove you trust this person?

2. In what kinds of relationships do you have the hardest time trusting others?
   - ☐ In my relationship with my parents
   - ☐ In my relationship with my teachers
   - ☐ In my relationships with the opposite sex
   - ☐ In one-on-one relationships
   - ☐ In groups like this one
   - ☐ Other: _____

3. What is it that makes you most afraid of trusting others?
   - ☐ I'm afraid of being made a fool of.
   - ☐ I'm afraid that others will talk about me behind my back.

☐ I'm afraid that people are two-faced.

☐ I'm afraid that others will take advantage of me.

☐ I'm afraid of emotionally investing myself in someone who will just leave me.

☐ Other: _____

4. Look around at the members of your small group. Whom do you trust? Why do you trust this person? Without saying his or her name, express to the group why you trust this person. Discuss the various reasons why a person is trusted in your small group. What is the consistent theme? How do you believe you rate as a person who can be trusted?

LARGE-GROUP TIME:
Turn to face the front for this teaching time. Follow along and take notes in your student book.

  **So What?** (30 minutes)

Real Trust

1. How does trust develop in a relationship?

2. What does real trust look like?

Learning from the Bible

Matthew 1:18-25

[18] The birth of Jesus Christ came about this way: After His mother Mary had been engaged to Joseph, it was discovered before they came together that she was pregnant by the Holy Spirit. [19] So her husband Joseph, being a righteous man, and not wanting to disgrace her publicly, decided to divorce her secretly.

[20] But after he had considered these things, an angel of the Lord suddenly appeared to him in a dream, saying, "Joseph son of David, don't be afraid to take Mary as your wife, because what has been conceived in her is by the Holy Spirit. [21] She will give birth to a son, and you are to name Him Jesus, because He will save His people from their sins."

[22] Now all this took place to fulfill what was spoken by the Lord through the prophet:

[23] See, the virgin will become pregnant
and give birth to a son,
and they will name Him Immanuel,

which is translated "God is with us."

[24] *When Joseph got up from sleeping, he did as the Lord's angel had commanded him. He married her [25] but did not know her intimately until she gave birth to a son. And he named Him Jesus.*

An Example of Real Trust

3. With what situation was Joseph faced?

4. Why do we want to take revenge on someone who has broken our trust?

5. Why should we leave revenge up to God?

6. On what grounds did Joseph have legitimate reason to give up on Mary?

7. What event occurred that helped Joseph reestablish trust with Mary?

The Choice to Trust

8. Was Mary showing a pattern of behavior or was this an isolated incident?

9. How has God demonstrated His willingness to trust mankind again?

10. How can we decide who is safe to trust?

 Do What? (15 minutes)

Making It Personal

1. When have you, like Joseph, felt as if someone you trusted betrayed you?

2. Considering all of Joseph's options, what would you have done had you been Joseph and there were no angel to tell you the truth of the situation?

3. Trust is one of the fundamental elements of a good friendship. What makes you trust your friends? What makes your friends trust you? Create a list with tips for building and maintaining trust in friendships. Three tips have already been provided. Complete the list by recording five more tips.
   1. Be honest with your friends.
   2. If your friends tell you a secret, keep it to yourself.
   3. Keep your promises, and don't make promises you can't keep.
   4.
   5.
   6.
   7.
   8.

 # LifePoint Review

Trust is one of the fundamental elements of a good relationship.

"Do" Points

These "Do" points will help you begin to experience this week's "LifePoint." Be open and honest as you discuss the action points within your small group.

1. <u>Talk through a situation where trust was strained with a person you now have trouble trusting.</u> Don't expect yourself just to start trusting someone again without having had the opportunity to come to some understanding about how trust was lost. Be careful to discuss the issue without letting your emotions run wild. Don't call the other person names or lay a heavy guilt trip on him or her. Just share how you felt at the time and how the incident affected you.

2. <u>Ask forgiveness of someone whose trust you have violated.</u> Most likely you've done something to cause someone else to stop trusting you. You will have to earn this person's trust back. Begin by approaching him or her with a real and honest

apology. Allow the person to explain how your actions made him or her feel. Let him or her know you are willing to take the necessary steps to reestablish trust in the relationship. Then be trustworthy! If your actions live up to your words, you will show this person that you can be trusted again.

3. <u>Ask a person you are having trouble trusting to do a small task for you.</u> Don't start with something big. Start with something that is important, but which will not have traumatic consequences if the person fails. Then gradually entrust bigger things to him or her. It's kind of like when an athlete gets injured and is put on a rehabilitation program. This may include a progressive plan of stretching and strengthening muscles. In baseball it often includes a "rehabilitation assignment" where the person plays on a minor league team, and the pressure isn't as high to perform. We can learn from this approach when our trust is "injured." We shouldn't expect to put that trust back into full operation all at once. We should have something like a "rehabilitation schedule" whereby we strengthen our trust and gradually put it back into full operation.

Prayer Connection:

This is the time for developing and expressing concern for each other. Lead group members to praise God for being so trustworthy in their lives. Ask Him to make each of them individuals who can be trusted. Guide group members to thank God for the trusted friends they have by calling out the names of these individuals and making specific requests on their behalf.

Share prayer needs and requests with the group, especially those related to hearing from and responding to God. Your group facilitator will close your time in prayer.

Prayer Needs:

Remember your
"Get Ready" daily
Bible readings
and questions at
the beginning of
session 5.

 # now What?

Trust is essential to true friendship. We all need someone with whom we can share our lives, our thoughts, and our feelings—both good and bad. We need to be able to share our deepest secrets with someone, without worrying that those secrets will be shared with others. Two good relationships in which we can develop such a high level of trust are with a mentor and with an accountability partner.

Option #1

A mentor is usually an older person who, through their experience and knowledge, can help and counsel you. A mentor will use his or her wisdom to show you how to best live out your faith. Individuals involved in this type of relationship meet on a regular basis. I believe my mentor could be: _____

Record the steps you will take to ask this individual if he or she will mentor you.

Option #2

An accountability partner is someone your age with similar standards and spiritual goals. You and your accountability partner pray for each other every day and stay in touch with each other on a regular basis. When you meet together you discuss what's going on in each of your spiritual lives and you encourage each other to be faithful to God. I believe my mentor could be: _____

Record the steps you will take to enlist this individual.

Bible Reference notes

Use these notes to gain further understanding of the text as you study on your own.

Matthew 1:18

engaged to Joseph. A first-century Jewish marriage had three parts to it: the engagement (this often took place when the couple were children and was usually arranged by a marriage broker); the betrothal (a one-year period in which the couple were considered virtually "married," though they did not have sexual relations); and the marriage. Mary and Joseph were at the second stage in their relationship.

she was pregnant. The penalty in the Old Testament for sleeping with a woman betrothed to another man was death by stoning for both parties (Deut. 22:23-24). By this time, however, the breaking of the engagement was the course that was usually followed.

by the Holy Spirit. Both Matthew and Luke made it quite clear that the agent in Jesus' birth was the Holy Spirit (Luke 1:35). In the Old Testament, the Spirit is often pictured as a creative force (Gen. 1:2; Ezek. 37:1-14) and, indeed, here the Spirit is at work bringing salvation to the world (Isa. 11:2; 42:1; 61:1; Joel 2:28).

Matthew 1:19

her husband. Although the marriage had not yet taken place, a betrothed couple were considered to be husband and wife.

righteous man. According to the Law, Joseph was required to break off his relationship with Mary (Deut. 24:1). However, out of compassion for her he decided not to do this publicly. He would not press charges against her as he had the legal right to do.

divorce. During betrothal, a divorce was required should either party wish to terminate the relationship.

secretly. To break off his engagement privately he would have needed only two witnesses.

Matthew 1:20-21

Luke records the visit of the angel to Mary; Matthew records the angelic visit to Joseph.

Matthew 1:20

a dream. Dreams were often the means by which God revealed Himself to people. Matthew records four other occasions when dreams were crucial during the birth and childhood of Jesus (2:12,13,19,22).

son of David. The crucial link between Joseph and David is made quite clear by the angel.

take Mary as your wife. The marriage was completed when the husband took his betrothed from her parents' home, where she lived during the betrothal, to his own home. Joseph needed to marry Mary in order for Jesus to become his legal son and share his lineage back to David.

Matthew 1:21

you are to name Him. It was necessary for Joseph to name Jesus and thus totally accept Him as his son.

Jesus. A common name. It is the Greek form of the Hebrew name Joshua, which means *God is salvation*. His name defines His mission.

He will save His people from their sins. It would not be His goal to establish a Jewish state in what was then Roman territory. Jesus did not come to be a warrior-messiah who would engage in battle against the oppressors of Israel; He would bring to humanity liberation from a far deeper problem—sin.

Matthew 1:22

prophet. This is the first of 10 instances where Matthew uses this formula (or one like it) to introduce a quotation from the Old Testament. In this way, Matthew points out the way in which Jesus fulfills Old Testament prophecy.

Matthew 1:23

The allusion is to Isaiah 7:14.

God is with us. The presence of God with His people is the climactic promise of God's covenant with Israel (Matt. 28:20).

Matthew 1:24-25

The marriage was completed, though not consummated until after the birth of Jesus.

MAKING FORGIVENESS REAL

 Get Ready

Read one of these short Bible passages each day, and spend a few minutes of focused time with God. Be sure to jot down any insights you receive.

MONDAY

Read Luke 15:11-16.

What are you squandering in your life right now? Who might feel bitter toward you for doing this?

TUESDAY

Read Luke 15:17-19.

When have you realized that you needed someone you thought you could do without? Will forgiveness be required to reestablish this relationship?

WEDNESDAY

Read Luke 15:20-21.

Why was the father able to approach his wayward son with forgiveness? How does God approach you when you return to Him?

THURSDAY

Read Luke 15:22-24.

What reunion have you celebrated the most in your life? Was forgiveness part of this reunion?

FRIDAY

Read Luke 15:25-30.

Are there areas in your life in which you are harboring bitterness? What has your bitterness accomplished?

Read Luke 15:31-32.

Has someone else extended forgiveness to you? How can you celebrate this forgiveness?

Read Luke 15:32.

Has God extended His forgiveness to you? How can you celebrate this forgiveness?

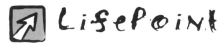 **LifePoiNt**

God's forgiveness of us models how we are to forgive others.

**SMALL-GROUP
TIME:**
Divide into
groups of four to
eight, preferably
in a circle
configuration. You
will have a small-
group leader for
"Say What?"

 **Say What?** (15 minutes)

Random Question of the Week:
If you had a garden, what would you plant in it?

Group Experience: Forgiveness
Answer the following questions and be prepared to share your responses.

1. Read and discuss this C.S. Lewis quote: We all agree that forgiveness is a beautiful idea until we have to practice it.

   Who in your life has forgiven you when you didn't expect it—or deserve it? How did this forgiveness make you feel?

2. Do you have a forgiving spirit? Circle the statement that best describes you:
   If people hurt me, I will get even.
   If I forgive people, I will look weak.
   God knows how bad people have hurt me. He doesn't expect me to forgive.
   I hold grudges for a very long time.
   It takes me awhile, but eventually I forgive.

I only forgive people if they ask. If they don't ask, I don't forgive.
My life is too short to hold a grudge. I forgive people immediately.
If God is willing to forgive me, I am willing to forgive others.

LARGE-GROUP TIME:
Turn to face the front for this teaching time. Follow along and take notes in your student book.

 # So What? (30 minutes)

Real Forgiveness

1. What does forgiveness have to be modeled after if it is to be true forgiveness?

2. What does it mean to have "false forgiveness"?

Learning from the Bible

Luke 15:11-32

[11] He also said, "A man had two sons. [12] The younger of them said to his father, 'Father, give me the share of the estate I have coming to me.' So he distributed the assets to them. [13] Not many days later, the younger son gathered together all he had and traveled to a distant country, where he squandered his estate in foolish living. [14] After he had spent everything, a severe famine struck that country, and he had nothing. [15] Then he went to work for one of the citizens of that country, who sent him into his fields to feed pigs. [16] He longed to eat his fill from the carob pods the pigs were eating, but no one would give him any. [17] When he came to his senses, he said, 'How many of my father's hired hands have more than enough food, and here I am dying of hunger! [18] I'll get up, go to my father, and say to him, Father, I have sinned against heaven and in your sight. [19] I'm no longer worthy to be called your son. Make me like one of your hired hands.' [20] So he got up and went to his father. But while the son was still a long way off, his father saw him and was filled with compassion. He ran, threw his arms around his neck, and kissed him. [21] The son said to him, 'Father, I have sinned against heaven and in your sight. I'm no longer worthy to be called your son.'

[22] "But the father told his slaves, 'Quick! Bring out the best robe and put it on him; put a ring on his finger and sandals on his feet. [23] Then bring the fattened calf and slaughter it, and let's celebrate with a feast, [24] because this son of mine was dead and is alive again; he was lost and is found!' So they began to celebrate.

[25] "Now his older son was in the field; as he came near the house, he heard music and dancing. [26] So he summoned one of the servants and asked what these things

meant. *27* 'Your brother is here,' he told him, 'and your father has slaughtered the fattened calf because he has him back safe and sound.'

28 "Then he became angry and didn't want to go in. So his father came out and pleaded with him. *29* But he replied to his father, 'Look, I have been slaving many years for you, and I have never disobeyed your orders, yet you never gave me a young goat so I could celebrate with my friends. *30* But when this son of yours came, who has devoured your assets with prostitutes, you slaughtered the fattened calf for him.'

31 " 'Son,' he said to him, 'you are always with me, and everything I have is yours. *32* But we had to celebrate and rejoice, because this brother of yours was dead and is alive again; he was lost and is found.' "

Cultural Background

3. Why was it an insult for the younger son to ask for his inheritance early?

4. How did the younger son further increase this offense against his father?

5. Why was being reduced to feeding pigs especially humiliating to this young man?

6. Why did the younger son decide to return home?

The Father's Forgiveness

7. What three things did the father not do in relation to his younger son's rebellion?

8. What was the meaning behind each of the gifts the father gives the prodigal upon his return?

9. What does this story teach us about our need for God's forgiveness?

Forgiving Each Other

10. What happens when we refuse to forgive?

11. How did the elder son show that he no longer thought of the younger son as his brother?

SMALL-GROUP
TIME:
Small-group
leaders will direct
your discussions.
Everyone will gain
more if you are
open and honest
in responding to
the questions.

Do What? (15 minutes)

Making It Personal

1. What would you have done had you been the father in this story?
   - ☐ Never let my son leave in the first place
   - ☐ Written to my son every day while he was away
   - ☐ Changed the locks on the house and not let my son back in
   - ☐ Made my son prove he was truly sorry before forgiving him
   - ☐ Stayed bitter for a long time
   - ☐ Forgiven him readily
   - ☐ Felt guilty about neglecting the elder son
   - ☐ Other: _____

2. What is your biggest barrier to showing forgiveness like the father showed in this story?
   - ☐ People haven't shown me that kind of forgiveness.
   - ☐ I struggle with feeling bitter over injustices done to me.
   - ☐ My own self-pity, which I can't seem to let go of
   - ☐ My fear of people taking advantage of me if I'm too forgiving
   - ☐ There are no barriers; I forgive readily because God forgave me.
   - ☐ Other: _____

3. Complete the following statements:
   Today, I am struggling with forgiving _____ for _____
   _____.
   I don't want to forgive this person because: _____.
   I believe that God is telling me to: _____.

LifePoint Review

God's forgiveness of us models how we are to forgive others.

"Do" Points

These "Do" points will help you begin to experience this week's "LifePoint." Be open and honest as you discuss the action points within your small group.

1. <u>Make a list of some of the things for which God has forgiven you.</u> Include big things as well as small things. Keep it in a confidential place. Consult it whenever you are having a hard time forgiving someone. Being thankful that God has forgiven you will encourage you to extend the same forgiveness to others.

2. <u>Talk about a deep hurt with a caring, trusted friend.</u> Forgiveness is the deliberate choice to release a person from any obligation they have toward you as a result of any offense they have committed against you. If you are having difficulty forgiving a hurt, sometimes it's because you haven't taken advantage of the healing that can come when you share your hurts with a trusted friend. Ask this person to continue praying for you until you have found the ability to forgive.

3. <u>Pray for God's forgiving love to fill you.</u> You can't do it on your own. When Corrie ten Boom, who spent some tough years in a Nazi prison camp for sheltering Jews, found herself faced with a former prison guard wanting forgiveness, she couldn't do it at first. Then she prayed, "Jesus, I cannot forgive him. Give me your forgiveness." She wrote, "As I took his hand the most incredible thing happened. From my shoulder along my arm and through my hand a current seemed to pass from me to him, while into my heart sprang a love for this stranger that almost overwhelmed me."[1] What you cannot do, God can do through you.

Prayer Connection:

Remember that this time is for developing and expressing your care for each other by sharing any personal prayer requests and praying for each other's needs. Pray that the group member to your right will be able, with God's strength, to overcome any barriers to forgiveness. Pray that the group member to your left will find the courage to ask for any needed forgiveness.

Share prayer needs and requests with the group, especially those related to hearing from and responding to God. Your group facilitator will close your time in prayer.

Prayer Needs:

Remember your
"Get Ready" daily
Bible readings
and questions at
the beginning of
session 6.

 # now What?

What can we do when forgiving is hard? Here are some actions we can take:

Option #1

Continue to discover Bible passages and stories that demonstrate God's love toward you. Here are some to get you started: Mark 11:25; Luke 7:36-50; Luke 15:1-10; Luke 17:4. Record any new insights you receive in your personal journal.

Option #2

Get "Five Steps to Forgiveness" from your leader and write them on a note card or your journal. Each time you are inclined to withhold forgiveness, review these steps.

5

Bible Reference notes

Use these notes to gain further understanding of the text as you study on your own.

Luke 15:12 *give me the share of the estate.* Under Jewish law, the younger of two sons was entitled to receive one-third of the estate upon his father's death (Deut. 21:17). While a father might divide up his property before he died if he wished, this son's request would be considered unbelievably callous and hard-hearted. In essence, he is saying that the fact his father was still alive was getting in the way of his plans. The father was under no obligation whatsoever to grant this request; the audience of the day would expect a father faced with such an insulting request to respond with anger. Instead, this father goes along with the request and gives his son the lawful inheritance.

Luke 15:13 *gathered together all he had.* In other words, the younger son sold off his share of the estate so that he could have cold, hard cash to do with as he wanted! Such an action would have been scandalous at a time when a person's identity and future were tied up with his family's land. For the sake of satisfying immediate pleasures, he separated himself from his family, threw away his means of income, and robbed any children he may have in the future of the security of owning land.

Luke 15:15 *sent him . . . to feed pigs.* Jews considered pigs to be ceremonially unclean animals (Lev. 11:7) and would not eat, raise, or touch them. There was even the pronouncement of a curse upon the person who cared for them.

Luke 15:16 *He longed to eat his fill from the carob pods the pigs were eating.* While eating the food of pigs sounds terrible even to modern readers, for the Pharisees in this audience it would have been utterly horrifying. Jesus painted a picture of an unbelievably arrogant, unpleasant, immoral, foolish, and irreligious young man.

Luke 15:19 *no longer worthy to be called your son.* The son realized that he had no legal, moral, or relational claim on his father's good will.
hired hands. These were day laborers employed only as the day-to-day work of the estate demanded.

Luke 15:20 Just as the actions of the son scandalized the Pharisees, so the response of the father violated their understanding of how such a son should be treated.

Luke 15:21

his father saw him. The implication is that the father had been waiting and hoping to one day see his son return.

was filled with compassion. There is no haughtiness of wounded pride, but only the welling up of pity, love, and joy.

He ran. Protocol and dignity were thrown to the wind as the father raced to his son. Social customs dictated that it was degrading for an elderly man to run to anyone, especially to someone who had disgraced him. This picture presents an absolutely unique, staggering insight into the response of the Almighty Holy God to a repentant sinner.

kissed him. While this was a typical greeting for men, it would have been thought inappropriate, given the son's grave offense against his father.

Luke 15:22

I'm no longer worthy to be called your son. Although the son may have thought he could earn his way back into some relationship with his father in order to alleviate his own misery, at this point he reflected a true sense of repentance: He could offer nothing except a contrite spirit (Ps. 51:17).

Luke 15:23

the best robe. This would have been the father's best robe. This is a sign that people should honor the son as they honor the father.

a ring. The signet ring gave the son the authority to represent the father.

sandals. Being shoeless was a sign of a slave. To wear shoes indicated a man was free to go where he pleased. Thus, the son was immediately and unconditionally elevated to a position of honor and respect in the home.

Luke 15:24

fattened calf. The fact that it was a calf that was prepared indicates that the whole village was invited to come to the feast (such provisions could feed 100 people).

Luke 15:28

was dead. It was as if the son was dead (he apparently had no intention to live in relationship with his father ever again).

The older son could only see that his father had violated all the customs of how such a wayward son should be treated. His refusal to enter the house would have been seen as a sign of grave disrespect, since the eldest son was expected to play the part of a gracious host at a family feast. As he did with the younger son, the father went out to plead with the older son. This, too, was an overwhelming display of grace since the son's refusal to come to the party was a serious social insult. The parable's listeners would have expected the father to be enraged.

Luke 15:29

Look. This would have been considered an extremely rude way for a son to address his father, since there is no hint of respect or affection.

I have been slaving many years for you. Ironically, this son viewed his ongoing relationship with his father in the way the younger son hoped he might be privileged to have on his return. While always in the vicinity of the father, the older son never enjoyed the relationship with his father that was available to him.

never disobeyed your orders. While there was the appearance of cooperation with the father, this son apparently viewed things in terms of a master/slave relationship. This reflected the Pharisees' reliance upon external conformity to God's law as the measure by which one could earn His blessing.

you never gave me. This observation ignores the fact that he had always been in the position to enjoy the love of his father, whereas the younger son had not.

Luke 15:31-32

We are not told what the older son did. Jesus left the story open-ended to force the Pharisees to fill in the ending by their behavior.

[1]Corrie ten Boom, *The Hiding Place* (Minneapolis, MN: World Wide Publications, 1971), 232–233.

Session 6

MAKING GOD'S LOVE REAL

 Get Ready

Read one of these short Bible passages each day, and spend a few minutes of focused time with God. Be sure to jot down any insights you receive.

MONDAY

Read Genesis 33:1-4.

Part of being in authentic relationships is taking the risk to be real and transparent with others. How did Jacob humble himself in the presence of Esau? Who are people in your life with whom you could take this kind of risk? Over what kind of issues have you wept with someone else?

TUESDAY

Read Genesis 33:5-7.

Jacob knew his family was a gracious gift from God. God chose to bless Jacob with his wives and his children. What are some things or who are some people God has graciously given to you?

WEDNESDAY

Read Genesis 33:8-9.

To find favor in his brother's eyes, Jacob brought gifts to Esau. What kinds of things are you doing to gain favor with your friends or family members? What kinds of things are you doing to try to find favor with God?

THURSDAY

Read Genesis 33:8-9.

Esau was more concerned about his brother than he was with receiving gifts. What is your primary concern in your relationships with friends and family members? Are you more concerned about them or about what they can do for you?

FRIDAY

Read Genesis 33:10-11.

Jacob said that seeing Esau was as precious as seeing the face of God. Who is someone you would be really excited to see today? What would it be like for you to be face to face with God?

SATURDAY

Read 1 John 4:12.

When we know God, we can express His love to others. How can you show someone God's love today?

SUNDAY

Read 1 John 4:20.

We can't say we love God, then turn around and hate another person. If we say we love God, we show it by loving others. What person or persons are you having the hardest time loving right now?

 # LifePoint

The act of giving and receiving forgiveness helps us to experience God's love.

SMALL-GROUP TIME:
Divide into groups of four to eight, preferably in a circle configuration. You will have a small-group leader for "Say What?"

 # Say What? (15 minutes)

Random Question of the Week:

What is the worst fight you remember having with a sibling or relative who is close to your age?

Group Experience: Forgiveness

Answer the following questions and be prepared to share your responses.

1. Which is easier for you to do?
☐ Ask someone else for forgiveness.
☐ Forgive someone else who has asked me to forgive them.
☐ Forgive someone who has never asked for forgiveness.
☐ Forgive myself.

2. Complete the following statements.
It is easier for me to forgive others when:

It is harder for me to forgive others when:

It is easier for me to feel forgiven when:

It is harder for me to feel forgiven when:

3. What is holding you back from mending a strained relationship in your life?
☐ I'm ready, they're not.
☐ They're ready, I'm not.
☐ It's too late, the relationship is ruined.
☐ The timing isn't right.
☐ The pain is too fresh.
☐ We are both still too hurt.
☐ I've already tried once before and been rejected.
☐ They've tried once before but I rejected their request for forgiveness.
☐ Other: _____

LARGE-GROUP TIME:
Turn to face the front for this teaching time. Follow along and take notes in your student book.

So What? (30 minutes)

The Face of God
1. What are some of the ways people seek God?

2. Why is it difficult to seek God while avoiding others with whom we have strained relationships?

3. What unique encounter did Jacob have with God?

4. To what earthly encounter did Jacob compare seeing God face to face?

Learning from the Bible

Genesis 33:1-11

¹ Now Jacob looked up and saw Esau coming toward him with 400 men. So he divided the children among Leah, Rachel, and the two female slaves. ² He put the female slaves first, Leah and her sons next, and Rachel and Joseph last. ³ He himself went on ahead and bowed to the ground seven times until he approached his brother.

⁴ But Esau ran to meet him, hugged him, threw his arms around him, and kissed him. Then they wept. ⁵ When Esau looked up and saw the women and children, he asked, "Who are these with you?"

He answered, "The children God has graciously given your servant." ⁶ Then the female slaves and their children approached him and bowed down. ⁷ Leah and her children also approached and bowed down, and then Joseph and Rachel approached and bowed down.

⁸ So Esau said, "What do you mean by this whole procession I met?"

"To find favor with you, my lord," he answered.

⁹ "I have enough, my brother," Esau replied. "Keep what you have."

¹⁰ But Jacob said, "No, please! If I have found favor with you, take this gift from my hand. For indeed, I have seen your face, and it is like seeing God's face, since you have accepted me. ¹¹ Please take my present that was brought to you, because God has been gracious to me and I have everything I need." So Jacob urged him until he accepted.

Encountering God in Private

5. What did Jacob name the place where he wrestled with God? Why did he choose this name?

6. Can you describe a time when you felt as if you had wrestled with God?

7. How do our private encounters with God affect our public encounters with others?

Encountering an Angry God
8. How did Jacob wrong Esau?

9. How have we wronged God?

10. When we come asking for forgiveness, how does God respond?

6

Encountering God in Each Other
11. Through what encounter did Jacob learn about the nature of God?

12. How can we reflect a loving and forgiving God to others?

 **Do What?** (15 minutes)

Making It Personal
1. If you were Jacob and looked up and saw Esau coming toward you with 400 men, what would you do?
   ☐ Arrange my wives and children according to which ones were my favorite
   ☐ Freeze up in fear
   ☐ Humble myself and bow down before Esau
   ☐ Scream like a little girl

☐ Run away
☐ Ask for Esau's forgiveness
☐ Cry out to God for protection from my angry brother
☐ March up to Esau, point my finger in his face, and say, "This is all your fault!"

How do you typically react when you see someone you have wronged?

2. If you were Esau, what would you do when you saw Jacob?
☐ Ignore him.
☐ Give him the silent treatment.
☐ Pretend like nothing was wrong.
☐ Run to give him a hug.
☐ Give him a piece of my mind.
☐ Tell my 400 guys to take him out.
☐ Forgive him.
☐ Make him squirm a little and then forgive him.
☐ Tell him, "I will never forgive you!"

How do you typically react when you see someone who has wronged you?

3. When you are feeling guilty about something you have done to someone, which of the following tactics are you most likely to use? (Check all that apply.)
☐ Send the person gifts to buy their favor.
☐ Send someone else to talk to the person for you.
☐ "Kiss up" to that person, saying nice things about him or her.
☐ Talk about everything except what you have done wrong.
☐ Send them a text or e-mail message asking for forgiveness.
☐ Talk to the person face to face about what you have done wrong.
☐ Other: _____

If you could go to someone from your past right now to ask for their forgiveness, who would it be?

4. How do you think this event affected Jacob and Esau's future relationship?
☐ It was probably just a temporary break in a lifetime of fighting.
☐ It gave them a good feeling about their relationship to hold onto when they were apart.

☐ It made for a more positive, caring relationship.

☐ Jacob probably did more things to hurt Esau just because he knew he could get away with it.

☐ Other: _____

How has forgiveness affected your relationships?

# LifePoint Review

The act of giving and receiving forgiveness helps us to experience God's love.

"Do" Points

These "Do" points will help you begin to experience this week's "LifePoint." Be open and honest as you discuss the action points within your small group.

1. <u>Before your next worship experience, take the initiative toward reconciliation of a conflict with someone.</u> In this study we have been focusing on authentic human relationships. This topic can't be isolated from our relationship with God. Our relationship with God affects how we relate to people and vice versa. Nowhere is this illustrated better than in the story of the reconciliation between Jacob and Esau. In Matthew 5:23-24, Jesus said, "So if you are offering your gift on the altar, and there you remember that your brother has something against you, leave your gift there in front of the altar. First go and be reconciled with your brother, and then come and offer your gift."

Think of the people with whom you worship God. Whose forgiveness do you need to request?

How can you get in touch with this person before your next worship experience?

What approach will you use to ask his or her forgiveness?

How will this affect your worship of God?

2. <u>If there are old hurts between yourself and a family member, seek reconciliation by calling, writing, or e-mailing.</u> Forgiveness is not just between friends or people with whom you worship God. It's also important for you to ask for forgiveness from members of your family. This may be the hardest relationship in which you will have to request forgiveness.

Why is it so difficult to ask forgiveness of a family member?

Think about your family members. Whose forgiveness do you need to request?

What approach will you use to ask his or her forgiveness?

How will this affect your family?

3. <u>Fill yourself with the biblical passages that urge forgiveness.</u> The more you learn about giving and receiving forgiveness, the more you will learn about making God's love real in your relationships with others. Read the following Bible verses about forgiveness. Scripture will keep the need to forgive constantly before your mind. Record any new insights you receive on forgiveness.
   Psalm 103:1-3:
   Matthew 6:12-15:
   Matthew 18:21-35:
   Ephesians 1:7-8:
   Ephesians 4:32:
   Colossians 3:13:

Prayer Connection:

This is the time for developing and expressing concern for each other. During this time, ask each group member to finish this sentence: Right now I need an "Esau" to forgive me for . . . . Pray for God's guidance and strength in responding to whatever needs are mentioned. Close by thanking God for bringing you together as a group and by asking Him to help you humbly request forgiveness where it is needed.

Share prayer needs and requests with the group, especially those related to hearing from and responding to God. Your group facilitator will close your time in prayer.

Prayer Needs:

Remember your "Get Ready" daily Bible readings and questions at the beginning of session 7.

 **now What?**

Most of us will not see an angel in this lifetime, as Jacob did at Peniel. But our experience with God can be just as real if we learn to show and receive the kind of forgiveness Esau gave to Jacob. Last week we gave some specific suggestions for steps to forgiveness. We need to apply those suggestions. This week, we want to look at some other suggestions on specific things we can do to connect love and forgiveness of others with experiencing the love of God.

Option #1

Jacob told Esau that seeing his face was like seeing the face of God, since he treated Jacob so well. When have you recently felt you experienced God's presence and love through the way someone treated you? As if you were writing in your personal journal, describe the experience on a sheet of paper.

When do you believe that you helped someone else experience God's presence and love through the way you treated them? Again, as if you were writing in your personal journal, describe the experience on a sheet of paper.

Option #2

In Exodus 33:17-23, Moses asked to see God's glory. Exodus 34:29 and 2 Corinthians 3:7-8 state that after seeing just a small part of God, Moses' face reflected God's glory. As Max Lucado stated it, "The brightness Moses saw was the brightness he became." Second Corinthians 3:18 states, "We all, with unveiled faces, are reflecting the glory of the Lord and are being transformed into the same image from glory to glory; this is from the Lord who is the Spirit." When you reflect His character, you make God's love real to others. You become "God with skin on" in their lives. When you give and receive forgiveness, you experience God's love.

This week, be aware of specific times when you feel like you are experiencing the presence of God in your life either by the way you treat someone or by the way they treat you. At the end of the week, record your experiences on a sheet of paper.

Bible Reference Notes

Use these notes to gain further understanding of the text as you study on your own.

Genesis 33:1-2

looked up and saw Esau. This was the first time Jacob had seen Esau since he had tricked him out of his blessing. Esau had vowed to kill Jacob in revenge after this incident (Gen. 27:41). The blessing and birthright were both considered vital to a person's success in the culture of the time.

toward him with 400 men. In this time before Israel had a national identity and army, local landowners and persons of prominence had armies of their own, consisting largely of family, friends, and hired help.

divided the children. Jacob had children by two wives, Leah and Rachel, as well as by their maidservants. In the culture of the time, when women were considered to be possessions (the wealthier you were, the more you possessed), this was considered acceptable behavior. Rachel was his most prized wife and Joseph his most prized child. He probably put them last to provide them the greatest protection in case Esau attacked.

Genesis 33:3

bowed to the ground seven times. Seven was a number that indicated perfection or completion. God completed creation in seven days. Here this act may indicate complete contrition. Similar acts of contrition and humility included Jacob's referring to Esau as "lord" (v. 8), and referring to himself as Esau's "servant" (v. 5).

Genesis 33:4

Esau ran to meet him. This scene is reminiscent of the story of the prodigal son, where the father ran to meet his son (Luke 15:11-32).

kissed him. This was a typical way for men who cared about each other to exchange greetings.

Genesis 33:8

whole procession. Jacob had sent some animals ahead as a gift to try to appease Esau (Gen. 32:13-16).

Genesis 33:10

like seeing God's face. Just prior to this story, Jacob had been alone in the desert and had wrestled with what he later learned was an angel of the Lord. He named the place where this happened "Peniel" (meaning *face of God*) because he felt he had seen God face to face. The experience of being loved and forgiven by his brother was on a par with that experience!

DEALING WITH REAL CONFLICTS

 ## Get Ready

Read one of these short Bible passages each day, and spend a few minutes of focused time with God. Be sure to jot down any insights you receive.

MONDAY

Read Luke 10:38.

Is your home open to other students from your youth group? How could you help to make your home a more welcoming place for your Christian friends? For your lost friends?

TUESDAY

Read Luke 10:39.

Mary stopped her chores and took time to sit at Jesus' feet and listen to His teaching. What time do you set aside to sit and listen "at the Lord's feet"?

WEDNESDAY

Read Luke 10:40.

While Mary sat at Jesus' feet, Martha was distracted by her duties in the kitchen. What responsibilities are distracting you right now from working on your spiritual growth?

THURSDAY

Read Luke 10:40-42.

What would Jesus say to you about the conflicts you are in right now with those around you? Would He take your side? Would He scold you for your behavior? Would He help you see both sides of the conflict?

FRIDAY

Read Luke 10:41-42.
Jesus said that learning from Him was the one thing on which both Mary and Martha needed to focus. What would Christ say to you about how well you are focusing on the "one thing" that is needed? If you are not focused on Him, what has become your "one thing"?

SATURDAY

Read Matthew 18:15.
Whom do you need to talk to right now about a conflict that has arisen?

SUNDAY

Read Matthew 18:16-17.
Have you tried everything possible to get that person in conflict with you to listen? If the person won't listen, what do you believe is your next step?

 # LifePoint

Biblical principles can be used to deal with conflicts in relationships.

SMALL-GROUP TIME:
Divide into groups of four to eight, preferably in a circle configuration. You will have a small-group leader for "Say What?"

 # Say What? (15 minutes)

Random Question of the Week:
Where would you like to spend your summer vacation and why?

Group Experience: Settling Conflict
Answer the following questions and be prepared to share your responses.

1. What are you most likely to get into a conflict about with your friends?
- ☐ Where you will sit at school for lunch
- ☐ Who gets to sit in the middle
- ☐ Who gets to ride in the front seat of the car
- ☐ Which movie you will see
- ☐ Borrowing each other's clothes
- ☐ Discussions about your beliefs
- ☐ Discussions about politics
- ☐ I never have any conflicts with my friends
- ☐ Other: _____

2. About what are you most likely to get into a conflict with members of your family?
- ☐ Using the bathroom first
- ☐ Riding in the front seat of the car
- ☐ Using the computer
- ☐ Eating the last cookie
- ☐ Choosing a TV program
- ☐ Choosing a radio station in the car
- ☐ Determining who made the mess in the kitchen
- ☐ Deciding whose job it is to feed a pet
- ☐ I never have any conflicts with members of my family.
- ☐ Other: _____

3. How do you typically deal with conflict with others?
- ☐ I give them the silent treatment.
- ☐ I get into a fist fight.
- ☐ I scream at them.
- ☐ I tell on them.
- ☐ I just try to forget about it.
- ☐ I walk away from them.
- ☐ I make them think I'm OK, but I get my revenge later.
- ☐ I try to make them see my side of the story.
- ☐ I try to consider their side of the story.
- ☐ I ask them to sit down and discuss the situation and try to come up with a compromise.

Does it make a difference if the conflict is a major or minor one?

 # So What? (30 minutes)

Conflicting Differences

1. How can our differences be good? How can our differences become a problem?

2. If Jesus were physically present, would all of our conflicts just go away?

The Inevitability of Conflict

3. Is it reasonable to believe that there will never be conflict in the church? Why or why not?

4. Why will there inevitably be conflict in the church?

Learning from the Bible

Luke 10:38-42

38 While they were traveling, He entered a village, and a woman named Martha welcomed Him into her home. 39 She had a sister named Mary, who also sat at the Lord's feet and was listening to what He said. 40 But Martha was distracted by her many tasks, and she came up and asked, "Lord, don't you care that my sister has left me to serve alone? So tell her to give me a hand."

41 The Lord answered her, "Martha, Martha, you are worried and upset about many things, 42 but one thing is necessary. Mary has made the right choice, and it will not be taken away from her."

Mary and Martha's Conflict

5. What may have attributed to the conflict between Mary and Martha?

A Process for Dealing with Conflict

6. What should be our first step in settling a conflict?

7. If the conflict is still not resolved after speaking privately with the other person, what could be the next step?

8. How could prayer be part of the conflict resolution process?

9. What might happen if we take our conflict to a person who is not involved in it?

When One Party Isn't a Christian

10. If our conflict is with someone who isn't a Christian, what are our options?

SMALL-GROUP
TIME:
Small-group
leaders will direct
your discussions.
Everyone will gain
more if you are
open and honest
in responding to
the questions.

 **Do What?** (15 minutes)

Making It Personal

1. Which of the following most reminds you of this story about Mary and Martha?
   - ☐ My relationship with my siblings—we fight over chores
   - ☐ My relationship with my friends right now—we have different priorities
   - ☐ Group projects at school—one person ends up doing the work while the others have fun
   - ☐ Youth group events—one leader seems to do all the work while the rest just sit around and watch
   - ☐ Other: _____

2. Comparing your personality to the two people in this story, which of them are you more like?

3. When you think something is unfair, to whom do you go to make things right?

4. How would you summarize Jesus' response to Martha?
   - ☐ "Martha, take a chill pill!"
   - ☐ "Martha, focus more on your spirit and less on your chores."
   - ☐ "Just be glad Mary has her spiritual priorities straight."
   - ☐ "Martha, you have to learn to put first things first."
   - ☐ Other: _____

5. If you had been Martha, how would you have responded to Jesus?
   - ☐ Talked to Mary privately about what needed to be done
   - ☐ Gone to my room and pouted
   - ☐ Sat at Jesus' feet along with Mary
   - ☐ Explained why I needed help
   - ☐ Asked Jesus to hold off teaching until dinner was ready
   - ☐ Let 'em all starve!
   - ☐ Just do the work and suffer silently
   - ☐ Sat down with Mary and let dinner burn
   - ☐ Gotten the work done ahead of time so I could sit and listen, too
   - ☐ I would have done just what Martha did
   - ☐ Other: _____

LifePoint Review

Biblical principles can be used to deal with conflicts in relationships.

"Do" Points

These "Do" points will help you begin to experience this week's "LifePoint." Be open and honest as you discuss the action points within your small group.

Many people who live in the same house readily identify with the story of Mary and Martha. Perhaps this is because there seems to be at least one "Mary" and one "Martha" in almost every living situation! However, even for those of us who do not readily identify with the kind of conflict Mary and Martha had, we can learn about handling the conflicts we do have. Having looked at the story of Mary and Martha and some other relevant Bible facts, here are some things we can actually do in order to better handle the conflict in our lives:

1. Discuss with the student pastor how conflict is handled in your youth group. Is there a group of adult or student leaders before whom conflicts can be taken? Should you take issues you have with another member of the youth group directly to your student pastor? Do your youth leaders simply try to ignore such conflicts, or do they leave such issues to be worked out by the students involved? Find out what is actually done, and how that compares to what your student pastor thinks should be done.

2. List anyone with whom you have a conflict and with whom you haven't talked to directly about that conflict. That is always the first step. Go through your list one at a time and talk to each individual about the conflicts that exist. Avoid casting blame. Try to listen to his or her side of the story. Concentrate on sharing what your feelings are and what you think might bring a solution that would satisfy everyone involved. End by thanking the person for discussing this conflict with you. Once a conflict is settled, don't keep bringing it up. Do your best to leave it alone.

3. Pray about your conflict situations. This should include prayer about approaching those individuals on your list and talking to them. It should also include prayer that Christ will reveal where your own misplaced priorities have contributed to these conflicts.

Prayer Connection:

This is the time for developing and expressing concern for each other. Take time now to care for one another through prayer. Go around the group and encourage each member to share one relational conflict they are having for which they need direction from God; then urge your group to pray for those conflicts. Take turns praying for one another, remembering the concerns that have been shared. Close by asking God to give each group member the wisdom to deal with their relational conflicts in an appropriate manner.

Share prayer needs and requests with the group, especially those related to hearing from and responding to God. Your group facilitator will close your time in prayer.

Prayer Needs:

Remember your
"Get Ready" daily
Bible readings
and questions at
the beginning of
session 8.

 ## now What?

Choose one of the following options to further examine Biblical principles that can be used to deal with conflicts in relationships.

Option #1
Jesus said Martha was "worried and upset about many things." What are you worried or upset about right now? Record three things here:

1.
2.
3.

Philippians 4:6-7 states, "Don't worry about anything, but in everything, through prayer and petition with thanksgiving, let your requests be made known to God. And the peace of God, which surpasses every thought, will guard your hearts and your minds in Christ Jesus."

First Peter 5:7 states, "casting all your care upon Him, because He cares about you."

How do these two passages give you perspective on the things that are worrying or upsetting you?

For further encouragement, read Matthew 6:25-34.

Option #2

In Luke 10:42, Jesus said, "but one thing is necessary. Mary has made the right choice, and it will not be taken away from her." Jesus was telling Martha, "Many things are important but only one thing is necessary." That one "necessary" thing was an intimate, authentic relationship with Him.

Read the following verses and record the "one thing" you are encouraged to focus on:
Psalm 27:4:

Philippians 3:13-14:

Hebrews 12:1-2:

What is distracting you from spending time with Jesus?

In what areas of your life do you need more balance so Jesus becomes your "one thing"?

What specific steps can you take to make your relationship with Jesus your first priority?

Bible Reference notes

Use these notes to gain further understanding of the text as you study on your own.

Luke 10:38

village. Bethany, just on the outskirts of Jerusalem, was the home of Martha and Mary and their brother Lazarus (whom Jesus raised from the dead).

a woman named Martha. Martha and Mary also appear in John 11:1-44, where their brother Lazarus died and was raised by Jesus. In that story it was Martha, rather than Mary, who was portrayed as the more faithful one. Martha opened her home to him. It appears that it was Martha's home (she was the head of the household), which explains why she felt more responsibility for the preparations.

Luke 10:40

my sister has left me to serve alone. This is a classic clash between a disciplined, task-oriented servant (Martha) and a more impulsive, person-oriented student (Mary). That Martha says Mary has left her to do all the work assumes the priority that work always comes first over learning and socialization. Martha emotionalized the issue by implying that those who don't share her priority "don't care." None of this is to say that Jesus "sided" against the more task-oriented person. He simply said that in this situation, with Jesus Himself present for a brief time, stopping to learn from Him should be the highest priority, and Mary chose that priority.

Luke 10:41

you are worried and upset. Martha was like the thorny soil in which the seed is choked by life's worries (Luke 8:14).

about many things. Martha's problem was an inability to focus her life around one central priority. As a result, she tried to be the "superwoman" who "does it all." Jesus calls us to focus our lives around the central priority of the kingdom of God, which then helps all other tasks and goals find their proper place (Matt. 6:25-34).

Luke 10:42

but one thing is necessary. Jesus is saying that listening and responding to the Word of the kingdom is the single most important thing in all of life. Mary had chosen to do that, rather than being distracted with the less important expectations of hospitality. Jesus gently commended that attitude to Martha who, in her zeal to "serve" Jesus, missed the importance of His presence and His words.

Session 8

BELIEVING IN REAL CHANGE

 Get Ready

Read one of these short Bible passages each day, and spend a few minutes of focused time with God. Be sure to jot down any insights you receive.

MONDAY

Read Acts 15:36.

Paul suggested that he and Barnabas go back and check on some of the churches they had helped to establish. What friend or friends do you need to check up on? In particular, do you have a new Christian friend who could use some encouragement in his or her fresh faith?

TUESDAY

Read Acts 15:37-39.

Paul and Barnabas got in a big fight over whether John Mark should accompany them on their next trip. When has a serious disagreement come between you and a friend? Do you still need to work on mending fences with this friend?

WEDNESDAY

Read Acts 15:40.

Because of their dispute, Paul and Barnabas split up, got new partners, and went to different places. What friend has come into your life to help fill a gap left by the loss of another friend?

THURSDAY

Read Acts 15:41.

The purpose of Paul's trip was to strengthen and encourage the churches he visited. What are you doing now to strengthen your church? What are you doing to encourage other students in your youth group? When was the last time you showed your support to your student pastor?

FRIDAY

Read 2 Corinthians 5:17.

Reflect on how Christ changed you when you became a Christian. What are some of the biggest changes He made in your life? Reflect on how you have seen Christ change your friends. What were the biggest changes you saw when a friend became a Christian?

SATURDAY

Read Romans 7:18-19.

Why is it so hard to change in our own power?

SUNDAY

Read Romans 7:24-25.

How has Christ helped you change the direction of your life?

 # LifePoint

Jesus gives people the ability to change.

SMALL-GROUP TIME:
Divide into groups of four to eight, preferably in a circle configuration. You will have a small-group leader for "Say What?"

 # Say What? (15 minutes)

Random Question of the Week:

What is one thing you would like to change about yourself?

Group Experience: Real Change

Answer the following questions and be prepared to share your responses.

1. In each of the following areas, record something about you that is different today than it was one year ago.
   Mentally:
   Physically:
   Emotionally:
   Relationally:
   Spiritually:

Why or how did these changes occur?

Which changes were real?

What part did Jesus have in bringing about these changes?

2. Make a list of three of your closest friends. Beside each of their names, record some significant changes you have seen in each of their lives.
   1.
   2.
   3.

   Why or how did these changes occur?

   Which changes were real?

   What part did Jesus have in bringing about these changes?

3. Think about someone who you've "written off" or don't want to have anything to do with because of the choices he or she has made. Do you believe that he or she could change? What part would Jesus need to have in bringing about these changes? Would you trust the changes?

   Using a code to represent this individual, record his or her name here:

   Write a brief prayer asking Jesus to help this person make the needed changes and to give you the ability to trust that these changes are real.

LARGE-GROUP TIME:
Turn to face the front for this teaching time. Follow along and take notes in your student book.

 So What? (30 minutes)

Real Change
1. How did God prove His willingness to help us change?

2. Why should Christians believe in Jesus' ability to help people change?

Learning from the Bible

Acts 15:36-41

36 After some time had passed, Paul said to Barnabas, "Let's go back and visit the brothers in every town where we have preached the message of the Lord, and see how they're doing." 37 Barnabas wanted to take along John Mark. 38 But Paul did not think it appropriate to take along this man who had deserted them in Pamphylia and had not gone on with them to the work. 39 There was such a sharp disagreement that they parted company, and Barnabas took Mark with him and sailed off to Cyprus. 40 Then Paul chose Silas and departed, after being commended to the grace of the Lord by the brothers. 41 He traveled through Syria and Cilicia, strengthening the churches.

The Failure of John Mark

3. What did John Mark do that disappointed Paul?

4. How did Barnabas and Paul respond to John Mark's decision to leave them?

5. What personal experience did Paul have that should have reminded him that people do change?

6. What was the result of the dispute between Paul and Barnabas?

How John Mark Changed

7. What evidence was there in John Mark's life that he truly had changed?

How Jesus Can Empower People to Change

8. What other biblical hero showed evidence of authentic change?

9. How does a person develop a cycle of failure?

10. How does Jesus break this cycle?

11. What is the only path to real change?

SMALL-GROUP TIME:
Small-group leaders will direct your discussions. Everyone will gain more if you are open and honest in responding to the questions.

 # Do What?

Making It Personal

1. What surprises you the most about this story?
   - ☐ That the Bible even talks about an argument between two famous church leaders
   - ☐ That a Christian leader like Paul was unwilling to forgive and forget
   - ☐ That Barnabas still trusted Mark after their previous experience
   - ☐ That Paul and Barnabas couldn't come to a better compromise
   - ☐ Other: _____

2. Who in your past stuck up for you when nobody else would?

3. When have you felt like someone let you down by not following through with a commitment he or she made to you?

4. In terms of how you normally act in situations like this one, where a decision needs to be made about trusting someone who has previously failed you, who are you more like?
   - ☐ Paul: Once bitten, twice shy. If people fail me, I may have trouble trusting them in the future.
   - ☐ Barnabas: Always believe the best about people. They may have failed me in the past, but I believe people can change.

5. Apparently, John Mark was able to change and stood with Paul in a time of need (Col. 4:10; 2 Tim. 4:11; Philem. 24). What do you see as the most relevant factors in helping people make that kind of change in their lives? Rank the following factors from 1 (least relevant) to 5 (most relevant):

___ People like Barnabas, believing in them and standing by them

___ People like Paul, not coddling them but making them reach for a higher standard

___ The maturity that comes with age

___ The power of Jesus Christ in their lives

___ The ability to learn from their mistakes

LifePoint Review

Jesus gives people the ability to change.

"Do" Points

These "Do" points will help you begin to experience this week's "LifePoint." Be open and honest as you discuss the action points within your small group.

It's one thing to believe in the abstract that people can change and that we should encourage that change. It's another thing entirely to put our trust in someone on the basis of the belief that real change has occurred. A classic *Peanuts* comic strip series illustrates this idea. Every year Lucy encouraged Charlie Brown to kick the football while she held it for him. Every year she pulled it away at the last second, sending him flying. He could believe that it was possible for Lucy to change, but could and should he believe it when she actually teed up the football?

Applying this week's session requires that we believe people can change, that we believe it enough, in fact, to run at that football one more time. Here are some specific things we can do to help put this kind of belief into action:

1. Make a list of positive changes you have made in your life over the last two years. Making this kind of list will help you see what God has done to help you change your own life, and that in turn, will help you believe that God is also working in the lives of others. (If your list turns out to be a little thin, it may also show you something about yourself!)

2. <u>Ask God to point you to people He is changing.</u> It is certainly true that not all people are open to change, and entrusting tasks to them could be foolish. But if we truly believe in God's guidance, then we can put our trust in that guidance into action by asking Him to make us aware of people who He is authentically changing.

3. <u>Choose one person to entrust with a task at which he or she has previously failed.</u> This might mean asking a friend who hasn't always been responsible in the past to help you with a favor. It might mean working on a school project with someone who always starts with great enthusiasm, but then doesn't always follow through. Remember, you're not doing this without God's help. You've prayed for guidance, now act on that guidance. Remember John Mark. Remember your own list. If the person fails you again, pray for more guidance. If the person succeeds, remember to affirm him or her.

Prayer Connection:
Take this time to encourage one another in prayer. Encourage group members to take turns answering the question, "In what ways do you feel you need to make a change like John Mark made?" Then have each person pray for the person to his or her left, remembering the changes that were shared.

Share prayer needs and requests with the group, especially those related to hearing from and responding to God. Your group facilitator will close your time in prayer.

Prayer Needs:

Remember your "Get Ready" daily Bible readings and questions at the beginning of session 9.

 ## now What?

Option #1
Take time to really focus on how Jesus changed your life by recording your personal testimony. Follow this outline by describing:

My life before I met Christ:
(What were you like? What kinds of choices did you make? Who were your friends?)

How I met Christ: (Who told you about a personal relationship you could have with Him? Why did you want to be in this relationship with Jesus? How did you enter into that relationship?)

My life since I met Christ: (What is your life like now? Are your choices different? Do you spend your time and money differently? Have your friendships changed?)

Option #2

Now that you have prepared your personal testimony, look for opportunities to share it with two people this week. Make the focus of your conversation about the change Jesus has made in your life. People may not agree with what the Bible states, but they can't argue with your story about the difference Jesus has made in your life. You might just share your story with someone who is looking for a change!

Bible Reference Notes

Use these notes to gain further understanding of the text as you study on your own.

Acts 15:36   *visit the brothers.* Paul was not a "fly-by-night" evangelist who arrived, "converted" people, then headed on his own way never to be heard from again. He had a deep concern for everyone he brought into the faith and was concerned that they thrive and grow as Christians. This is why he decided to go back and visit them.

Acts 15:37   *take along John Mark.* He was the author of the Gospel of Mark and a cousin of Barnabas (Col. 4:10). His mother's home was apparently an important house church in Jerusalem since it was where the disciples met to pray for Peter's release when he was imprisoned (Acts 12:12).

Acts 15:38   *who had deserted them.* While the word used to describe Mark's leaving in Acts 13:13 is a neutral one that implies nothing negative, the word used here is related to the word for *apostasy*. Luke does not tell us why Mark left, but Paul certainly viewed it as a serious deficit and was unwilling to let him try again.

Acts 15:39-40   *a sharp disagreement.* This is a strong word used in the Septuagint version of the Old Testament to describe God's anger at the idolatry of Israel (Deut. 29:28; Jer. 32:37). Barnabas' concern may have been motivated in part by the fact that Mark was his cousin (Col. 4:10), but it is characteristic of Barnabas. Years before, it was he who insisted that Paul be given a chance to prove himself to the apostles (Acts 9:27) and recognized Paul's gifts for ministry (Acts 11:25-26). On the other hand, Paul was concerned about the immediate needs and demands of such a rigorous journey. Undoubtedly, Mark's eager departure placed increased demands on Paul and Barnabas, and he was unwilling to risk that again. While the action focuses on Paul and Silas, Barnabas and Mark also left Antioch on a missionary trip as they returned to Cyprus (Acts 13:4-12). Early church tradition teaches that Barnabas remained there until his death. Paul's letters reveal that he and Barnabas were later reconciled (Col. 4:10) and that Mark was counted by Paul as a valuable assistant (Col. 4:10; 2 Tim. 4:11; Philem. 24).

Acts 15:41   Whereas the limits of Paul's first journey were reached by an overland trek westward to the border of Cilicia, this time he went east, going overland through the provinces until he came to Derbe (Acts 16:1; Acts 14:20). Thus, the last community he visited on his earlier journey was the first to be visited on his second journey.

FINDING REAL MENTORS

 Get Ready

Read one of these short Bible passages each day, and spend a few minutes of focused time with God. Be sure to jot down any insights you receive.

MONDAY

Read 2 Kings 2:1-2.
Elisha promised Elijah that he would stay by the prophet's side. Who can you count on to be by your side at all costs?

TUESDAY

Read 2 Kings 2:3-6.
How prepared are you for the loss of people who are nearest to you?

WEDNESDAY

Read 2 Kings 2:7-8.
What "river" blocks the path to where you feel called to go in life?

THURSDAY

Read 2 Kings 2:8.
Who has taught you the most about dealing with the obstacles in your path?

FRIDAY **Read 2 Kings 2:9-10.**

What are some of the expectations you have of your friends? What are their expectations of you? Do your friends sometimes make difficult requests of you? How do you respond?

SATURDAY **Read 2 Kings 2:11-12.**

Can you recall a time when you were separated from a close friend? What was your response? When might God have separated you from a close friend so you could grow?

SUNDAY **Read 2 Kings 2:13-15a.**

What skills or characteristics have you received by being in authentic relationships with others?

 # LifePoint

Mentoring relationships can make valuable contributions toward spiritual growth.

SMALL-GROUP TIME:

Divide into groups of four to eight, preferably in a circle configuration. You will have a small-group leader for "Say What?"

 # Say What? (15 minutes)

Random Question of the Week:

What secret skill or ability do you have that others in your group may not know about?

Group Experience: Real Mentors

Answer the following questions and be prepared to share your responses.

1. Who is a famous person you admire? What skill or characteristic do they have that you would like to have too?

2. Who is a "regular" person in your life you admire? What skill or characteristic do they have that you would like to have too?

3. What individual has contributed the most toward your spiritual growth? What contributions have they made?

4. How would you define the word *mentor?* Check all of the following descriptions you believe define the role of a mentor:

☐ A wise advisor
☐ A trusted counselor, guide, or teacher
☐ A buddy
☐ A coach
☐ An influential person who advises another individual
☐ An assigned, formal relationship between a more mature person and a less experienced person
☐ A person who gives recommendations to someone about a decision or choice he or she needs to make
☐ Other: _____

LARGE-GROUP TIME:
Turn to face the front for this teaching time. Follow along and take notes in your student book.

 **So What?** (30 minutes)

Direction and Inspiration

1. In what areas do people typically desire a mentor?

2. What are some biblical examples that illustrate what it means to be in a mentoring relationship?

Learning from the Bible

2 Kings 2:1-15

¹ The time had come for the Lord to take Elijah up to heaven in a whirlwind. Elijah and Elisha were traveling from Gilgal, ² and Elijah said to Elisha, "Stay here; the Lord is sending me on to Bethel."

But Elisha replied, "As the Lord lives and as you yourself live, I will not leave you." So they went down to Bethel.

³ Then the sons of the prophets who were at Bethel came out to Elisha and said, "Do you know that today the Lord will take your master away from you?"

He said, "Yes, I know. Be quiet."

⁴ Elijah said to him, "Elisha, stay here; the Lord is sending me to Jericho."

But Elisha said, "As the Lord lives and as you yourself live, I will not leave you." So they went to Jericho.

⁵ Then the sons of the prophets who were in Jericho came up to Elisha and said, "Do you know that today the Lord will take your master away from you?"

He said, "Yes, I know. Be quiet."

⁶ Elijah said to him, "Stay here; the Lord is sending me to the Jordan."

But Elisha said, "As the Lord lives and as you yourself live, I will not leave you." So the two of them went on.

⁷ Fifty men from the sons of the prophets came and stood facing them from a distance while the two of them stood by the Jordan. ⁸ Elijah took his mantle, rolled it up, and struck the waters, which parted to the right and left. Then the two of them crossed over on dry ground. ⁹ After they had crossed over, Elijah said to Elisha, "Tell me what I can do for you before I am taken from you."

So Elisha answered, "Please, let there be a double portion of your spirit on me."

¹⁰ Elijah replied, "You have asked for something difficult. If you see me being taken from you, you will have it. If not, you won't."

¹¹ As they continued walking and talking, a chariot of fire with horses of fire suddenly appeared and separated the two of them. Then Elijah went up into heaven in the whirlwind. ¹² As Elisha watched, he kept crying out, "My father, my father, the chariots and horsemen of Israel!" Then he never saw Elijah again. He took hold of his own clothes and tore them into two pieces.

¹³ *Elisha picked up the mantle that had fallen off Elijah and went back and stood on the bank of the Jordan. ¹⁴ Then he took the mantle Elijah had dropped and struck the waters. "Where is the LORD God of Elijah?" he asked. He struck the waters himself, and they parted to the right and the left, and Elisha crossed over.*

¹⁵ *When the sons of the prophets from Jericho, who were facing him, saw him, they said, "The spirit of Elijah rests on Elisha." They came to meet him and bowed down to the ground in front of him.*

Choosing the Mentoring Relationship

3. Where did Elijah find Elisha?

4. What are some good guidelines for selecting a mentor?

Elisha's Commitment

5. What is one of the central features of Elisha's relationship to Elijah?

6. What finally separated Elisha and Elijah?

A Temporary Relationship

7. About what did the prophets warn Elisha?

8. About what did Jesus warn His disciples?

9. Why can't the mentoring relationship last forever?

The Roles of Mentor and Mentoree

10. What are the roles of a mentor and the mentoree?

11. What is the goal of a mentoring relationship?

12. What did Elisha learn from Elijah?

SMALL-GROUP TIME:

Small-group leaders will direct your discussions. Everyone will gain more if you are open and honest in responding to the questions.

 Do What? (15 minutes)

Making It Personal

1. What surprises you most in this story?
   - ☐ Everyone seems to know what is going to happen to Elijah.
   - ☐ Elijah and Elisha were able to travel so far in one day.
   - ☐ Elijah is able to pass his miraculous power on to Elisha.
   - ☐ Elijah always seems to be trying to leave Elisha behind.
   - ☐ Other: _____

2. What do you see as the most influential factor in Elisha being able to take on the power of Elijah?
   - ☐ Elisha's persistence in sticking by Elijah everywhere he went, even being present at Elijah's ascent to heaven (v. 11)
   - ☐ Elisha picking up Elijah's cloak (vv. 13-14)
   - ☐ Elisha learning about what it means to follow God's lead (vv. 2,4,6)
   - ☐ Other: _____

3. Which of the following do you see as most critical to a mentoring relationship, such as existed between Elijah and Elisha?
☐ Loyalty, such as Elisha showed (vv. 2,4,6)
☐ A mentor who truly wants to help the person he or she is mentoring (v. 9)
☐ A love between the mentor and mentoree that is like parent and child (v. 12)
☐ The willingness to follow your mentor anywhere (vv. 2,4,6)
☐ The ability of the person mentored to observe the mentor in action (vv. 8,14)

 # LifePoint Review

Mentoring relationships can make valuable contributions toward spiritual growth.

"Do" Points

These "Do" points will help you begin to experience this week's "LifePoint." Be open and honest as you discuss the action points within your small group.

In this session, what action you should take depends on where you are in your spiritual journey. Maybe you need to have a mentor. Maybe you need to think in terms of someone you can mentor. Or maybe you can take on both roles at the same time—mentoring someone who is younger and needing direction, while at the same time having a mentor who helps you learn the next steps in your spiritual journey.

Needing a Mentor:
1. Make a list of qualities you need in a mentor. You might want to start by reviewing Fred Smith's list from the presentation in "Choosing the Mentoring Relationship." However, make sure to add qualities relevant to your own personality and needs.

2. Go to your student pastor and ask if he knows people with the qualities you have listed as important in a mentor. Ask your student pastor to suggest at least two people who might qualify to be your mentor. These people don't have to be from your own church, but they do need to be people he highly recommends.

3. Choose one individual and make an appointment to talk to him or her about mentoring. Don't expect a final decision right away, but leave it as something the two of you will pray about.

Ready to Mentor:

1. <u>Ask your student pastor or a mature Christian who knows you well, whether he or she sees you as qualified to mentor.</u> If so, ask him or her what kind of person he or she sees you working with best. A spiritual gifts inventory might also help you decide this since you would want to find someone who needs someone with your gifts.

2. <u>Go to your student pastor or other youth leaders and ask for names of younger students who need a mentor.</u> These should be younger students who are at a point in their lives where they might be ready for such a relationship, not simply someone who "needs help."

3. <u>Choose one individual and set up a time to talk to him or her about mentoring.</u> Share what you have learned in this session and why you chose to talk to him or her. Don't expect a final decision right away, but leave it as something the two of you will pray about. Be aware that many churches wisely require some kind of screening process for anyone wishing to work with youth.

Prayer Connection:

Use this time to pray for one another. Ask for God's discernment and guidance in choosing a mentor or in choosing whether or not to become a mentor. Close by thanking God for those who have served as mentors to persons in the group.

Share prayer needs and requests with the group, especially those related to hearing from and responding to God. Your group facilitator will close your time in prayer.

Prayer Needs:

Remember your
"Get Ready" daily
Bible readings
and questions at
the beginning of
session 10.

 # now What?

Choose one of the following options to further develop your mentoring relationships.

Option #1

You may not have the time or the maturity level to be in an assigned, formal mentoring relationship. However, the children's program at your church most likely needs volunteers to help with the kids' program. Volunteer to help in their Sunday School, their Wednesday night program, or at special programming like kids' camp or Vacation Bible School. Watch for opportunities to set a good example for the children of your church. Encourage the children you meet to grow up in their relationship with Jesus.

Option #2

This session is a good reminder of the people who have taught you various things along your spiritual journey. Take time this week to send each of these people a thank-you note. In these notes, express your gratefulness for what they have brought into your life.

9

Bible Reference Notes

Use these notes to gain further understanding of the text as you study on your own.

2 Kings 2:1 *whirlwind.* The coming of God is often associated with a strong wind. (See Isa. 29:6; 40:24; Ezek. 13:11; Zech. 9:14; Acts 2:1-2.)

2 Kings 2:3 *sons of the prophets.* The prophets of a given locale were joined in somewhat of a fraternal relationship. All of these, along with prophets at Jericho (v. 5) and probably the Jordan (v. 7), seemed to be aware that Elijah would depart this world in a special way.

2 Kings 2:8 *struck the waters, which parted.* This scene is reminiscent of the parting of the Red Sea (Ex. 14:15-31), as well as the crossing of the Jordan when the people of Israel originally entered the promised land (Josh. 3). It would have been seen as an evidence of God's presence with Elijah.

2 Kings 2:9 *a double portion.* A man's firstborn son received a double portion of his inheritance—twice as much as other sons would receive (Deut. 21:15-17). This does not mean twice as much as Elijah himself had. While Elisha was not biologically Elijah's son, he was his spiritual son. So what he is asking is not part of Elijah's physical inheritance, but something much more valuable to him—his spiritual inheritance.

2 Kings 2:10 *If you see me.* This required both Elisha's loyalty, that he stick around until that time, as well as his perception, that he be able to see the spiritual portents, such as the chariots of fire from heaven. Only the spiritually discerning could see such things (2 Kings 6:17).

2 Kings 2:11 *separated the two of them.* Elisha had already shown that he would never voluntarily leave the side of his mentor, and so it took an act of God to separate Elisha from Elijah's side. Elijah went up to heaven. The representation here is that Elijah did not actually die, but was taken directly to heaven. While Jewish tradition held the same had been true of Moses, Deuteronomy 34:5 said he actually died. Of no other character in Scripture is it said that he or she went directly to heaven without dying, and this was a tribute to Elijah's great spiritual stature. Because of this special way of departing, it was later said that Elijah would first return as a sign of the coming of the Messiah. Elijah joined Moses to be with Jesus on the Mount of Transfiguration (Matt. 17:1-13).

2 Kings 2:12 *Elisha watched.* This fulfilled the requirement put upon him by Elijah in verse 10.
took hold of his own clothes and tore them into two pieces. This was a sign of mourning.

2 Kings 2:13 *Elisha picked up the mantle.* Some of the power of such a great man of faith was felt to be transferred to his clothing. We see this again with Jesus when a woman with a hemorrhage decided that if she just touched the hem of Jesus' garment, she would be healed (Matt. 9:20-21).

2 Kings 2:14 *where is the Lord God of Elijah?* One of the drawbacks of having such a great person of faith around is people can get the idea that once that person is gone, God will no longer be able to do great things. Elisha here shows that the God of Elijah is still alive and well! This is reminiscent of how Jesus later said of the one who follows Him, "And he will do even greater works than these, because I am going to the Father" (John 14:12).

[1]Fred Smith, "Mentoring that Matters," *Leadership* (Winter, 1999), Vol. XX, No. 1, 98.
[2]Ibid., 95–98.
[3]Ibid., 95.

REAL EQUITY

 Get Ready

Read one of these short Bible passages each day, and spend a few minutes of focused time with God. Be sure to jot down any insights you receive.

MONDAY

Read Philemon 4-5.

Whom do you especially thank God for right now? Why are you thankful for this individual?

TUESDAY

Read Philemon 6-7.

In what ways are you encouraging other believers? In what ways are other believers encouraging you?

WEDNESDAY

Read Philemon 8-11.

What friends do you have who are as close or closer to you than family?

10

THURSDAY

Read Philemon 12-16.

When has God used separation to make you even closer to a friend or loved one?

FRIDAY

Read Philemon 17-21.

To which of your friends do you feel you owe a favor? Why do you believe you owe him or her this favor?

SATURDAY

Read Galatians 3:28.

In Jesus Christ, we are all considered equal. What group of people or what type of individual do you sometimes have trouble seeing your "oneness" with, even when they are in Christ? Do you look down on any other Christians?

SUNDAY

Read James 2:1-4.

Have you ever been treated differently based solely on your appearance? Have you ever treated someone differently based on their perceived difference from you? Are you sometimes guilty of showing favoritism to a certain type of person?

 LifePoint

All believers have equal status as brothers and sisters in the family of God.

SMALL-GROUP TIME:
Divide into groups of four to eight, preferably in a circle configuration. You will have a small-group leader for "Say What?"

 Say What? (15 minutes)

Random Questions of the Week:

How many classes do you have with your best friend?

Group Experience: Real Equity

Answer the following questions and be prepared to share your responses.

1. Who is a non-family member who is like a brother or sister to you? What qualities does this person have that make you see him or her in this way? Do you have anyone whom you feel this way about who others might think is from a different social status than you?

2. Which of the following factors are most influential in determining who feels like a brother or sister to you?
   - ☐ Similar interests
   - ☐ Similar beliefs
   - ☐ Similar life experiences
   - ☐ Honest communication
   - ☐ Sharing the same space together and learning to get along
   - ☐ Other: _____

3. Which of the following has been most likely to separate you from someone you felt was like a brother or sister to you?
   - ☐ One of our families moved.
   - ☐ One of us changed to a different school or to a different church.
   - ☐ We no longer participated in the same extra-curricular activities.
   - ☐ One of us made the team, and one of us did not.
   - ☐ We didn't have any classes together at school.
   - ☐ We had a rivalry over a member of the opposite sex.
   - ☐ We just grew in different directions.
   - ☐ One of us lost interest in the relationship.
   - ☐ Other: _____

10

LARGE-GROUP
TIME:
Turn to face the
front for this
teaching time.
Follow along and
take notes in your
student book.

 # So What? (30 minutes)

Created Equal

1. On what principle was the United States founded?

2. What are some groups who were not originally included in this principle?

Learning from the Bible

Philemon 4-21

⁴ I always thank my God when I mention you in my prayers, ⁵ because I hear of your love and faith toward the Lord Jesus and for all the saints. ⁶ I pray that your participation in the faith may become effective through knowing every good thing that is in us for the glory of Christ. ⁷ For I have great joy and encouragement from your love, because the hearts of the saints have been refreshed through you, brother.

⁸ For this reason, although I have great boldness in Christ to command you to do what is right, ⁹ I appeal, instead, on the basis of love. I, Paul, as an elderly man and now also as a prisoner of Christ Jesus, ¹⁰ appeal to you for my child, whom I fathered while in chains—Onesimus. ¹¹ Once he was useless to you, but now he is useful to both you and me. ¹² I am sending him—a part of myself—back to you. ¹³ I wanted to keep him with me, so that in my imprisonment for the gospel he might serve me in your place. ¹⁴ But I didn't want to do anything without your consent, so that your good deed might not be out of obligation, but of your own free will. ¹⁵ For perhaps this is why he was separated from you for a brief time, so that you might get him back permanently, ¹⁶ no longer as a slave, but more than a slave—as a dearly loved brother. This is especially so to me, but even more to you, both in the flesh and in the Lord.

¹⁷ So if you consider me a partner, accept him as you would me. ¹⁸ And if he has wronged you in any way, or owes you anything, charge that to my account. ¹⁹ I, Paul, write this with my own hand: I will repay it—not to mention to you that you owe me even your own self. ²⁰ Yes, brother, may I have joy from you in the Lord; refresh my heart in Christ. ²¹ Since I am confident of your obedience, I am writing to you, knowing that you will do even more than I say.

Revolutionary Transformation

3. How did Jesus revolutionize the standing of women?

4. How did Jesus demonstrate that Gentiles were equal to Jews?

5. How did Jesus change people's perception of slaves?

6. How did Paul sum up Jesus' revolutionary transformation?

Background to the Story

7. How were Onesimus, Philemon, and Paul connected?

8. How did Paul use the word "brother" and what did it indicate?

10

Words of Transformation

9. Why might it be better for Philemon to have Onesimus as a brother rather than as a slave?

10. What is the meaning of Onesimus' name and how did his life change in the way he demonstrated this meaning?

11. From where does our equality come?

SMALL-GROUP TIME:
Small-group leaders will direct your discussions. Everyone will gain more if you are open and honest in responding to the questions.

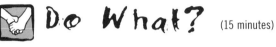 **Do What?** (15 minutes)

Making It Personal

1. What impression do you get of Paul from how he handled this matter of Onesimus and his relationship to Philemon?
   ☐ Paul really knew how to take someone on a guilt trip!
   ☐ Paul knew how to be a strong advocate for someone else.
   ☐ Paul believed in the equality of all people.
   ☐ Paul wasn't an activist for societal change since he never mentioned the issue of slavery.
   ☐ Other: _____

2. What do you sometimes allow to separate you from other Christian students your age?
   ☐ Social status
   ☐ Intelligence
   ☐ Athletic ability
   ☐ Level of popularity
   ☐ Looks
   ☐ Where they live
   ☐ What kind of clothes they wear
   ☐ What their parents do for a living
   ☐ Where they go to church
   ☐ The choices they make
   ☐ Popularity
   ☐ Other: _____

3. What makes you feel like you are better than others? How does understanding that we are all equals in Christ change your attitude?

4. What makes you feel like you are inferior? How does understanding that we are all equals in Christ change your attitude?

 # LifePoint Review

All believers have equal status as brothers and sisters in the family of God.

"Do" Points

These "Do" points will help you begin to experience this week's "LifePoint." Be open and honest as you discuss the action points within your small group.

To truly believe that all people are equal in the sight of God is not to say it but to act it. That is what we must now resolve to do. Whenever we ignore someone in a service profession or act like they exist to serve us, our behavior says that we think we are better than him or her. Whenever we make fun of someone with a disability, our behavior says that we think we are better than him or her. Whenever we put down someone else's accomplishment because we don't think it measures up to our own accomplishments, our behavior says we believe in our own superiority.

Applying this week's session means to start treating everyone as a person of worth who can contribute by serving God in his or her own way. Here are some specific things you can do to help put this kind of belief into action:

1. Focus this week on affirming people who truly are serving others in the church. This may be the janitor who ensures that the church is clean before every service. It may be the church secretary or one of the preschool workers. Let them know that you appreciate what they do.

2. Discuss with three different people, in three different stations in life, how they see God using them. One may be a grocery store bagger. Perhaps one will be a retired teacher. Still another might be an executive at a corporation. It would be best to choose people who have been Christians for awhile, so that they have enough maturity about them to share in this way. How are these three alike? How is God using them in different ways?

10

3. <u>Make it a point this week to truly listen to another Christian to whom you are not accustomed to listening.</u> By listening, you are affirming him or her as a person with something to say; that he or she is a person of worth. What can you learn from this person whom you are not used to listening to? How is he or she like you? How can you set aside your differences and treat him or her as an equal?

Prayer Connection:

This is the time for developing and expressing concern for each other. Use this time to share prayer requests and to pray for one another. Instruct each person in the group to share how someone served him or her in this past week. Pray that all of those people can some day be brothers and sisters in Christ.

Share prayer needs and requests with the group, especially those related to hearing from and responding to God. Your group facilitator will close your time in prayer.

Prayer Needs:

Remember your
"Get Ready" daily
Bible readings
and questions at
the beginning of
session 11.

 now What?

Choose one of the following options to further reinforce the idea that all believers have equal status as brothers and sisters in the family of God.

Option #1

Paul provided a good example of how to deal with a possible conflict between Christian friends. Paul based his request not on his own authority, but on Philemon's Christian commitment. For whom might you serve as a "Paul" in bringing about reconciliation? What are some specific words and attitudes that Paul used that will help you to bring these two individuals together?

Option #2

You will know you are making strides in your understanding of true equity among all people when you step outside of your typical comfort zone and instigate a new relationship with someone to whom you formerly felt either superior or inferior. Think specifically of an individual with whom you could establish such a relationship. Consider why you either felt inferior or superior to this person. How does understanding that you are equal in Christ motivate you to reach out to this person? What steps will you take to enter into a "like a brother or sister" relationship with him or her?

Bible Reference notes

10

Use these notes to gain further understanding of the text as you study on your own.

Philemon 5 *love . . . faith.* While Paul often used some combination of the triad of faith, hope, and love in his letters, the emphasis here falls upon the love God expects to be demonstrated between Christians.

Philemon 6 *participation in the faith.* Literally, *your fellowship of the faith.* This is not a prayer for fruitfulness of some type of evangelistic activity, but a desire that Philemon's participation in the faith would continue to be actively expressed by his good deeds.

may become effective through knowing every good thing that is in us for the glory of Christ. Participation in Christ requires believers to behave toward others with the same goodness that Christ has shown them.

Philemon 7	**hearts of the saints have been refreshed.** As Philemon had encouraged the hearts of so many others, Paul would appeal to him to "refresh my heart" (v. 20) by receiving Onesimus as a brother.
Philemon 8-21	Since a slave revolt would greatly threaten Roman social and economic conditions, disobedient and runaway slaves were punished severely as a deterrent to others.
Philemon 8-9	**on the basis of love.** Christian love, not a grudging obedience to Paul's command, was the only basis on which a true brotherly relationship could be built between Philemon and Onesimus.
	elderly man ... prisoner. While not appealing to his apostolic authority, Paul certainly appealed to the respect Philemon has for him! Paul's stress on his imprisonment (vv. 1,9,23) may be a hint that he, too, knew the limitations of a form of enslavement.
Philemon 10	**my child.** Onesimus became a Christian through Paul's ministry. Paul elsewhere spoke of his converts as his children (1 Cor. 4:15,17; Gal. 4:19; Phil. 2:22; 1 Thess. 2:7,11).
Philemon 11	**useless ... useful.** There is a play on words here. These two words, which sound very similar in Greek, share a root word that was pronounced the same way as the word for "Christ" (*christos* means *Christ*; *chestos* means *useful*). Through Christ, Onesimus (whose name means *useful*), formerly a useless, disobedient slave, has now become truly useful as a brother in the Lord.
Philemon 12	In spite of his love, Paul had to send Onesimus back since harboring a runaway slave was a serious crime. The reality of his conversion would be seen in his willingness to return to Philemon and face up to the consequences of what he had done. Christian slaves were expected to view their work for their master as working for the Lord (Col. 3:22-25). This does not mean that Christianity condones slavery as a legitimate institution, but, given the social order of the time, this was a way for individual Christian slaves to express their loyalty for Christ within the limits imposed upon them.
Philemon 16	**as a dearly loved brother.** Literally, *in the flesh and in the Lord.* "In the flesh" Onesimus was just a slave, but "in the Lord" he was now Philemon's spiritual brother.
Philemon 17	**partner.** While Paul does not request Philemon to release Onesimus from slavery, ultimately it is this vision of love and equality between all Christians that undermines the oppression of slavery, economic oppression, or social injustice.
Philemon 18	Onesimus may have stolen some money before running away. Besides that, his escape caused economic loss through lost services.
Philemon 19	**with my own hand.** Paul most generally wrote the body of his letters through a secretary (Rom. 16:22), but then he often wrote personal notes at the end of his letters with his own hand (1 Cor. 16:21; Gal. 6:11; Col. 4:18; 2 Thess. 3:17). Here, writing with his own hand is probably a reassurance that he will pay Philemon back for his financial losses.

GIVING REAL SUPPORT

 ## Get Ready

Read one of these short Bible passages each day, and spend a few minutes of focused time with God. Be sure to jot down any insights you receive.

MONDAY **Read Job 2:11-12.**

How often have you been willing to leave the comfort of your home to go comfort a friend? When was the last time you did so? When was the last time someone did this for you?

TUESDAY **Read Job 2:13.**

How comfortable are you just sitting and being silent with a friend who is having a difficult time? Have you ever wished that people would just sit quietly with you rather than give you advice?

WEDNESDAY **Read Job 6:14.**

Who has been there to help you at times when you felt abandoned by God? How did this individual help you?

THURSDAY **Read Job 6:15-20.**

Reflect on a time when you felt disappointed by the way your friends showed true support for you. What can you learn from this about being a supportive friend?

FRIDAY **Read Job 6:21.**

What fears do you have that keep you from truly being supportive of your friends?

Read 2 Timothy 4:16-17.

Have you ever felt God giving you strength when no human friend supported you? How is God's support different than the support of your friends?

Read Philippians 4:14-19.

What have you done to show your thanks to friends who supported you when you needed them?

 # LifePoint

In times of crisis, real support comes from being present, sensitive, and careful with our words.

SMALL-GROUP TIME:
Divide into groups of four to eight, preferably in a circle configuration. You will have a small-group leader for "Say What?"

 # Say What? (15 minutes)

Random Questions of the Week:

Would you rather be the best player on the worst team or the worst player on the best team? Why?

Group Experience: Giving Real Support

Answer the following questions and be prepared to share your responses.

1. If you were to choose three friends to come and be with you while you were going through hard times, whom would you choose and why? (You can choose people you actually know, famous people, or fictional people.)

   1.
   2.
   3.

2. What is the closest you have come to going through a time of despair like Job was going through?

3. Who or what helped you get through the time you referred to in question 2?

4. Of all of your friends, which one is able to comfort you the most when you are going through a difficult time? What does this friend do or not do that brings you such comfort?

LARGE-GROUP TIME:
Turn to face the front for this teaching time. Follow along and take notes in your student book.

 ## So What? (30 minutes)

You've Got a Friend
1. What did Job lose?

2. How did Job's wife respond to this loss?

3. How did Job's friends respond to his trouble?

Learning from the Bible

Job 2:11-13;
6:14-21

[11] *Now when Job's three friends—Eliphaz the Temanite, Bildad the Shuhite, and Zophar the Naamathite—heard about all this adversity that had happened to him, each of them came from his home. They met together to go and offer sympathy and comfort to him.* [12] *When they looked from a distance, they could barely recognize him. They wept aloud, and each man tore his robe and threw dust into the air and on his head.* [13] *Then they sat on the ground with him seven days and nights, but no one spoke a word to him because they saw that his suffering was very intense.*

¹⁴ *A despairing man should receive loyalty from his friends,*
even if he abandons the fear of the Almighty.
¹⁵ *My brothers are as treacherous as a wadi,*
as seasonal streams that overflow.
¹⁶ *and become darkened because of ice,*
and the snow melts into them.
¹⁷ *The wadis evaporate in warm weather;*
they disappear from their channels in hot weather.
¹⁸ *Caravans turn away from their routes,*
go up into the desert, and perish.
¹⁹ *The caravans of Tema look for these streams.*
The traveling merchants of Sheba hope for them.
²⁰ *They are ashamed because they had been confident of finding water.*
When they arrive there, they are frustrated.
²¹ *So this is what you have now become to me.*
When you see something dreadful, you are afraid.

What Job's Friends Did Well

4. What is the first thing Job's friends did well?

5. What is the second thing Job's friends did well?

6. What is the third thing Job's friends did well?

What Job's Friends Did Not Do Well

7. Of what did Job's friends accuse him and his family?

8. On what belief did Job's friends base their accusations?

9. What explanation did Jesus give to explain why people have struggles?

10. What was God's opinion of Job and of Job's three friends?

Supporting a Friend

11. What is the main thing we should consider when we want to be a supportive friend?

SMALL-GROUP
TIME:
Small-group
leaders will direct
your discussions.
Everyone will gain
more if you are
open and honest
in responding to
the questions.

 **Do What?** (15 minutes)

Making It Personal

1. Had you been one of Job's friends in this story, what would you have done or said to help him?

2. When bad things happen to good people, whom do you blame?

3. Job compared his friends to unreliable, intermittent streams that ceased to flow in the dry, hot season. To what would you compare your friends who have tried to be supportive of you?
   ☐ The same—intermittent streams
   ☐ More like a dry river bed that hasn't seen water in years!
   ☐ What friends?
   ☐ A deep, cool, refreshing mountain stream
   ☐ A deep river—but totally polluted!
   ☐ Other: _____

4. Job said, "A despairing man should receive loyalty from his friends, even if he abandons the fear of the Almighty" (6:14). What do you see as the most important thing a friend can do for someone who is struggling with God?

5. When do you believe silence can be more preferable, even more powerful, than words?

LifePoint Review

In times of crisis, real support comes from being present, sensitive, and careful with our words.

"Do" Points

These "Do" points will help you begin to experience this week's "LifePoint." Be open and honest as you discuss the action points within your small group.

Fortunately, few of us have friends who have gone through as much tragedy as Job did. But all of us have friends who are going through hard times. Perhaps it's a death in the family. Maybe it's the loss of their parent's job or the prospect of their parent's divorce. Maybe it's illness. In all such situations, we need to be present as a supportive friend. We need to avoid the mistakes of Job's friends while understanding what they did do right. Here are some specific suggestions to help us do that:

1. <u>Analyze your own experience in troubled times.</u> What is the closest you have come to going through a time like Job went through? What helped you most during this time and what helped you least? Who showed themselves to be genuine friends?

2. <u>Interview a couple of your friends about difficult times they have gone through.</u> What happened to them, and what helped them recover? Find out what other people did that was helpful and what people did that was not helpful. In what respect was their experience like and unlike the experience of Job?

3. <u>Ask your pastor or a member of your church staff for the name of another Christian going through difficulties, who might enjoy a visitor.</u> While visiting this person, resolve to listen to them and learn as much as you can about the experience they are going through. Avoid any temptation you might have to give unsolicited advice, condemnation, or to lecture or teach the person going through this difficult time.

Prayer Connection:

This is the time for developing and expressing concern for each other. During this time, encourage everyone in the group to finish the sentence: "The thing I could most use the support of friends in dealing with right now is . . ." Go around the group and invite each person to pray for the person on his or her right, using the "Prayer Needs" listed. Start with this sentence: Dear God, I thank You for my friend

_____.

Close by thanking God for bringing you together as a group and by asking Him to give you the strength and wisdom to be a supportive friend.

Prayer Needs:

Remember your "Get Ready" daily Bible readings and questions at the beginning of session 12.

 # now What?

Option #1

In *Job: A Man of Heroic Endurance*, Charles Swindoll's book about the life of Job, he provides words of advice about how to react to a friend's struggle. Copy this list into your personal journal or onto a note card. Use it as a reminder of how to behave whenever you are called on to be a supportive friend. (If you're curious about the life of Job and want to understand more about his experience, this might be a great book for you to read.)

1. Friends care enough to come without being asked to come.
2. Friends respond with sympathy and comfort.
3. Friends openly express the depth of their feelings.
4. Friends aren't turned off by distasteful sights.
5. Friends understand, so they say very little.

Option #2

Today, you have probably already thought of a friend who is in the midst of a struggle and could use some real support. Record your friend's struggle here:

Based on what you learned today, record three specific things you believe you could do to be supportive of your friend. Beside each, list how and when you will show your friend this support.

1.
2.
3.

Bible Reference Notes

Use these notes to gain further understanding of the text as you study on your own.

Job 2:11   ***all this adversity that had happened to him.*** These included loss of his livestock, servants, and finally his children in a series of catastrophes (Job 1:6-22). Then he developed a painful skin disease (Job 2:1-10).

Job 2:12   ***could barely recognize him.*** This could have been from the disfiguring aspects of the skin disease or from the effects of his deep mourning.

tore his robe and threw dust into the air and on his head. These acts were traditional signs of mourning in this culture. (See Lam. 2:10; Matt. 26:65.)

Job 2:13   ***sat on the ground.*** This was another sign of mourning. (See 2 Sam. 12:16.)

seven days and nights. Since creation was finished in six days, seven was considered to be a number of completion.

no one spoke a word. They had enough understanding to realize that sometimes when a person is mourning, what he or she needs most is the quiet presence of friends. They understood what Solomon later wrote in Ecclesiastes, that there is "a time to be silent" (Eccl. 3:7b). Unfortunately, they then started talking, and undid their good work! They blamed Job's misfortune on him, saying it must be some kind of punishment for unrighteous behavior (4:7-9; 8:4-7; 11:13-20).

Job 6:14   ***if he abandons the fear of the Almighty.*** A person of faith should not turn away from a friend who has turned from God. Such action would probably only harden the person even more against God. Sticking by a person in such a time may be God's way of bringing the individual back to Him. In fact, Job had not turned against God. However, he was saying that even if that were to happen, his friends should stick by him.

Job 6:15-17   ***as treacherous as a wadi.*** In a dry land like Israel, a reliable source of water was vital. But many streams, called "wadis" were formed by mountain run-off in the spring, then dried up in the hottest part of the summer when they were needed the most. Job was saying that his friends were like such wadis. When things "heated up" for him, they were not true friends. In Isaiah 48:18, God similarly promises that the peace He gives will be as reliable as a river, rather than an unreliable wadi.

Job 6:20   ***they had been confident.*** They thought they were OK because they knew where water was, having seen it before. But when they came to the place where the water had been, the stream had dried up. Job felt like he had similarly relied on friends, thinking they would be there for him, but they weren't.

SHOWING REAL CONFIDENCE

 ## Get Ready

Read one of these short Bible passages each day, and spend a few minutes of focused time with God. Be sure to jot down any insights you receive.

MONDAY   **Read 2 Timothy 1:1-4.**

Which of your friends do you remember in prayer on a daily basis? What do you pray for this friend? Why is it important for you to pray for your friends?

TUESDAY   **Read 2 Timothy 1:5-6.**

What unique gifts do you believe God has given to your friends? How do you see your friends using those gifts?

WEDNESDAY   **Read 2 Timothy 1:7.**

Do you feel like you are living your life in a spirit of fear? How would your life change if you lived it with the power, love, and self-discipline God has provided?

THURSDAY   **Read 2 Timothy 1:8.**

Do you have friends who are so strong in their Christian faith that sometimes you are embarrassed when you are in public with them? How can you be encouraged by their boldness?

12

Read 2 Timothy 1:8-12.

How willingly do you take on the suffering that sometimes comes with standing up for Christ?

Read 2 Timothy 1:12

How firmly convinced are you right now of the reality of Jesus Christ? Does your life demonstrate your faith in Him?

Read 2 Timothy 1:13-14.

Whose faith can you look to as a pattern for your own spiritual life? Are you relying on the Holy Spirit to help you live your faith with confidence?

 # LifePoiNt

We are to help each other find our gifts and encourage each other to use those gifts.

SMALL-GROUP TIME:
Divide into groups of four to eight, preferably in a circle configuration. You will have a small-group leader for "Say What?"

 # Say What? (15 minutes)

Random Questions of the Week:
How old were you when you learned to talk? walk?

Group Experience: Showing Real Confidence
Answer the following questions and be prepared to share your responses.

1. Who are some people who passed the Christian faith on to you? Was it a parent or grandparent, as we will see with Timothy, or a friend or teacher? What did this

person say or do that was most influential? How did they encourage you to be bold in your own faith?

2. In this session, we will study how the apostle Paul affirmed the spiritual gifts of a young preacher named Timothy. What are some of the spiritual gifts others have said they see in you? Do you think they are right? In what ways do you already use these gifts?

3. What would it mean for you to "fan into flame" the gifts you mentioned in question 2?
- ☐ To use them more
- ☐ To develop them more through training
- ☐ To discover new ways to use them
- ☐ To use them for God, instead of just personal need or ambition
- ☐ To have more confidence in using them
- ☐ Other: _____

LARGE-GROUP TIME:
Turn to face the front for this teaching time. Follow along and take notes in your student book.

 # So What? (30 minutes)

The Seed of Potential
1. How did Paul demonstrate his confidence in Timothy?

2. What is our task as a church?

Learning from the Bible

2 Timothy 1:1-14

¹ Paul, an apostle of Christ Jesus by God's will, for the promise of life in Christ Jesus:

² To Timothy, my dearly loved child.

Grace, mercy, and peace from God the Father and Christ Jesus our Lord.

³ I thank God, whom I serve with a clear conscience as my forefathers did, when I constantly remember you in my prayers night and day. ⁴ Remembering your tears, I long to see you so that I may be filled with joy, ⁵ clearly recalling your sincere faith that first lived in your grandmother Lois, then in your mother Eunice, and that I am convinced is in you also.

⁶ Therefore, I remind you to keep ablaze the gift of God that is in you through the laying on of my hands. ⁷ For God has not given us a spirit of fearfulness, but one of power, love, and sound judgement.

⁸ So don't be ashamed of the testimony about our Lord, or of me His prisoner. Instead, share in suffering for the gospel, relying on the power of God,

⁹ who has saved us and called us with a holy calling,
not according to our works, but according to His own purpose and grace,
which was given to us in Christ Jesus before time began.
¹⁰ This has now been made evident
through the appearing of our Savior Christ Jesus, who has abolished death
and has brought life and immortality to light through the gospel.

¹¹ For this gospel I was appointed a herald, apostle, and teacher, ¹² and that is why I suffer these things. But I am not ashamed, because I know whom I have believed and am persuaded that He is able to guard what has been entrusted to me until that day.

¹³ Hold on to the pattern of sound teaching that you have heard from me, in the faith and love that are in Christ Jesus. ¹⁴ Guard through the Holy Spirit who lives in us, that good thing entrusted to you.

Sharing Confidence Through Words

3. What did Paul say to encourage Timothy's faith?

4. What did Jesus say to encourage His disciples' faith?

5. To what gift of Timothy's was Paul referring?

6. To what did Paul compare Christians who believe they have no special gifts?

7. What did Paul urge Timothy to do with his spiritual gifts?

8. Who would help Timothy use his gifts?

Showing Confidence Through Action
9. How did Paul prove his confidence in Timothy?

10. What are some other indications of Paul's confidence in Timothy?

11. How can we show confidence through our actions?

SMALL-GROUP
TIME:

Small-group
leaders will direct
your discussions.
Everyone will gain
more if you are
open and honest
in responding to
the questions.

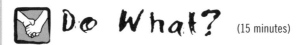

Do What? (15 minutes)

Making It Personal

1. From reading this part of Paul's letter to Timothy, how confident would you say Paul was in Timothy as a disciple?

   ☐ Not at all
   ☐ A little
   ☐ Mixed
   ☐ Quite confident
   ☐ Totally confident

2. If you were Timothy, which of the things Paul said would do the most to increase your confidence?

   ☐ Paul's affirmation of my faith (v. 5)
   ☐ Paul's reminder that the Holy Spirit is the source of my gifts (vv. 6-7)
   ☐ Paul's reminder that success doesn't rest on my ability but on the power and grace of God (vv. 8-10)
   ☐ Paul's own firm confidence in Christ (v. 12)

3. Why do you think Paul expressed these thoughts to Timothy?

   ☐ To help him feel better about himself
   ☐ To spur him on to even greater things
   ☐ To set him up to do Paul a favor
   ☐ To flatter him in order to keep Timothy on his side
   ☐ Other: _____

4. Who are the family or friends (like Lois and Eunice for Timothy) who have inspired you to faith? Have you had a spiritual mentor like Paul? How has the confidence of these individuals affected your own confidence?

5. Imagine that you truly put aside your "spirit of timidity" and acted in real confidence. How would you use your gifts in service to God and for others?

 LifePoint Review

We are to help each other find our gifts and encourage each other to use those gifts.

"Do" Points

These "Do" points will help you begin to experience this week's "LifePoint." Be open and honest as you discuss the action points within your small group.

As Paul showed confidence in Timothy through his actions as well as his words, so must we if our show of confidence is to be real. Saying that we believe in someone's ability isn't enough if we still insist on doing things ourselves that we could delegate to him or her. For instance, the parent who does a child's science project so it will be done "right" essentially tells that child the parent has little confidence in him or her, regardless of their words.

Here are some specific things we can do to show confidence in others through both words and actions:

1. <u>Teach a child a new skill this week and give him or her a chance to use that skill.</u> This could be anything from making a craft, to understanding how to play a game, to learning how to use a computer program. Make sure the task is age appropriate. Give the child something specific to make or do. You can supervise but give as little help as possible—coach from the sidelines.

2. <u>Identify a younger teen in your youth group to whom you can teach a task or ministry that you have traditionally done.</u> You might take that student with you to work in the children's ministry or have him or her help you with setup before a youth group event. Teach the individual how you do it, then let him or her try it alone. Give reassurance with verbal expressions of confidence.

3. <u>Identify someone in your youth group who seems to lack confidence and share with him or her what Paul wrote to Timothy.</u> Emphasize especially verses 6 and 7. Help that person to discover the gifts he or she has been given so they can be "kept ablaze."

12

Prayer Connection:

Remember that this time is for developing and expressing your care for each other by sharing any personal prayer requests and praying for each other's needs. During this time, have each person in the group finish the statement, "An area where I could use more confidence is . . ." Then pray that God will strengthen your group members in the areas they mentioned.

Share prayer needs and requests with the group, especially those related to hearing from and responding to God. Your group facilitator will close your time in prayer.

Prayer Needs:

Remember your "Get Ready" daily Bible readings and questions at the beginning of session 13.

 now What?

Option #1

This lesson probably made you curious about spiritual gifts. Do you know what your spiritual gifts are? Do you know how to use them in your church? You can take an online spiritual gift assessment at *http://www.lifeway.com/lwc/files/lwcF_PDF_Discover_Your_Spiritual_Gifts.pdf*. Get together with a group of close friends and take this test. Share the results of your tests. Discuss the evidence you see of your friends' spiritual gifts. Encourage them to use their gifts. Allow your friends to do the same for you. Share the results of your assessment with your youth pastor. Ask him to give you opportunities to use your spiritual gifts.

Option #2

Use this session as an opportunity to be "Paul" to a "Timothy." Select individuals in your life who need someone to see their potential and to cheer them on to bigger and better things. Be the person in their life who helps to instill confidence. In the same way that Paul wrote Timothy a letter, choose two people to whom you can send a letter that challenges and encourages them in their faith and in the use of their gifts.

Bible Reference notes

Use these notes to gain further understanding of the text as you study on your own.

2 Timothy 1:1 — *an apostle of Christ Jesus.* At first glance it is surprising that Paul used his title in such a personal letter. However, as in 1 Timothy, he was making his appeal in this letter as an apostle. This time his appeal was to Timothy. Paul urged him in strong terms to maintain his loyalty to him and the gospel, despite the suffering this might entail. There may be a second reason Paul used his title. This letter would probably be read by others. In particular, Timothy would need to show it to the elders in Ephesus when he told them that Paul wanted him to leave and go to Rome.

2 Timothy 1:3 — *I constantly remember you.* Paul prayed regularly, and in those prayers he always remembered Timothy.

2 Timothy 1:4 — *Remembering your tears.* Paul was probably remembering when they parted the last time, he to go on to Macedonia, while Timothy stayed in Ephesus. (See Acts 20:37 for a similar situation.)

I long to see you. This is the main reason Paul wrote this letter, to urge Timothy to join him (2 Tim. 4:9).

joy. Once again, as he did in Philippians, Paul sounded a note of joy even though he was in prison.

2 Timothy 1:5 — *Eunice.* Timothy's mother was a Jewish Christian. His father was a Gentile (a Greek), who probably was not a believer (Acts 16:1).

2 Timothy 1:6 — *keep ablaze.* Rekindle. Paul used the image of a fire, not to suggest that the gift of ministry has "gone out," but that it needs constant stirring so it always burns brightly.

the gift of God. Paul reminded Timothy not only of his spiritual roots (the faith of his mother and grandmother), but of the gift (*charisma* in Greek) he was given for ministry.

2 Timothy 1:7 — *fearfulness.* Some people are naturally shyer than others, and Timothy was probably shyer than the outspoken Paul. Paul said that even a shy person does not need to be ruled by timidity or fears in regard to acting for Christ because God empowers us to do more than we would be able to do naturally.

power, love, and sound judgement. The Spirit in Timothy led not to "timidity" but to these positive characteristics.

12

2 Timothy 1:8

ashamed of the testimony about our Lord. The gospel message about a dying Savior was not popular in the first-century world. The Greeks laughed at the idea that the Messiah could be a convicted criminal and that God was so weak He would allow His own Son to die. And the Jews could not conceive of a Messiah (whom they knew to be all-powerful) dying on a cross (which they felt disqualified Him from acceptance by God). It was not easy to preach the gospel in the face of such scorn.

or of me. When Paul was rearrested, his friends deserted him (2 Tim. 1:15). He did not want Timothy to do the same.

His prisoner. Paul may have been in a Roman jail, but he knew he was not a prisoner of Caesar. He was, and had long been, a willing prisoner of Jesus. (See Eph. 3:1; 4:1; Philem. 1, 9.)

share. In fact, rather than being ashamed of the gospel (or of Paul and his suffering), Timothy ought to share in his suffering.

suffering. Paul understood from his own experience (and that of Jesus) that suffering is part of what it means to follow the gospel. (See Rom. 8:17; 2 Cor. 4:7-15; Phil. 1:12,29; Col. 1:24; 1 Thess. 1:6; 2:14; 3:4; 2 Tim. 3:12.)

2 Timothy 1:9

has saved us. Timothy could face suffering because he had already experienced salvation. This was an accomplished fact.

grace. God's work of salvation depends wholly on "grace" (His unmerited favor lavished on His creation), not "according to our works." This grace, which was in place "before time began," is "given us in Christ Jesus" (See Eph. 1:4).

2 Timothy 1:10

appearing. The Greek word is *epiphaneia* (from which the English word epiphany is derived). It refers here to the manifestation of God's grace via the incarnation of Christ.

death . . . life. Jesus' work of salvation is described in His two-fold act of destroying the power of death over people (death no longer has the final word) and bringing resurrection life in its place.

2 Timothy 1:12

I am not ashamed. The fact that he was in prison brought no shame to Paul, despite how others viewed it.

2 Timothy 1:14

In words paralleling verse 12 and 1 Timothy 6:20, Paul urged Timothy to preserve faithfully the "sound teaching" of the gospel.

Session

13

REAL GREATNESS

 Get Ready

Read one of these short Bible passages each day, and spend a few minutes of focused time with God. Be sure to jot down any insights you receive.

MONDAY

Read Matthew 20:20-21.
If you could ask Jesus just one favor, what would it be?

TUESDAY

Read Matthew 20:22-23.
What "cup" or common experience of hard times have you shared with a friend? How has that affected your friendship?

WEDNESDAY

Read Matthew 20:24.
When have you done something that made your friends annoyed or put out with you? How did they respond to you?

THURSDAY

Read Matthew 20:25.
In what ways have you recently tried to "be the boss" of your friends? How did they respond?

13

FRIDAY   **Read Matthew 20:26-27.**

What have you done in the past few weeks that was an act of service to one of your friends? How did they respond? How did you feel after performing this act of service?

SATURDAY   **Read Matthew 20:28.**

How do you know Jesus loves you? What example did He set with His life?

SUNDAY   **Read Philippians 2:3-11.**

What must it have been like for Jesus to leave His place in heaven and take on the humble form of a human? What does His example teach you?

 # LifePoint

Real greatness comes through personal sacrifice and servanthood.

SMALL-GROUP TIME:
Divide into groups of four to eight, preferably in a circle configuration. You will have a small-group leader for "Say What?"

 # Say What? (15 minutes)

Random Question of the Week:
In what ways have your parents embarrassed you?

Group Experience: Real Greatness
Answer the following questions and be prepared to share your responses.

1. Who are some of the greatest people you know? What makes them so great? What standard did you apply to them to determine that they are great?

2. Let's try to define what a truly "great person" is. Check all of the following statements that you believe indicate a person is demonstrating signs of greatness.
   - ☐ Can slam dunk a basketball
   - ☐ Is a millionaire
   - ☐ Owns a lot of cars
   - ☐ Works at a homeless shelter
   - ☐ Takes care of an elderly, sick parent
   - ☐ Wears all the latest fashions to school
   - ☐ Is a talented singer and dancer
   - ☐ Makes straight A's
   - ☐ Puts others' needs before their own
   - ☐ Has lots of people working for them
   - ☐ Gives up his or her dreams in order to become a missionary
   - ☐ Is willing to suffer for his or her faith in Christ
   - ☐ Other: _____

3. Has it ever occurred to you that you could be a great person by serving others? How is this different from the world's definition of greatness?

LARGE-GROUP TIME:
Turn to face the front for this teaching time. Follow along and take notes in your student book.

 So What? (30 minutes)

13

The Key to Success
1. What are some ways our culture pursues greatness?

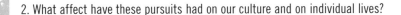

2. What affect have these pursuits had on our culture and on individual lives?

3. Where does true greatness come from?

Learning from the Bible

Matthew 20:20-28

[20] *Then the mother of Zebedee's sons approached Him with her sons. She knelt down ask Him for something.* [21] *"What do you want?" He asked her.*

"Promise," she said to Him, "that these two sons of mine may sit, one on Your right and the other on Your left, in Your kingdom."

[22] *But Jesus answered, "You don't know what you're asking. Are you able to drink the cup that I am about to drink?"*

"We are able," they said to Him.

[23] *He told them, "You will indeed drink My cup. But to sit at My right and left is not Mine to give; instead, it belongs to those for whom it has been prepared by My Father."* [24] *When the 10 disciples heard this, they became indignant with the two brothers.* [25] *But Jesus called them over and said, "You know that the rulers of the Gentiles dominate them, and the men of high position exercise power over them.* [26] *It must not be like that among you. On the contrary, whoever wants to become great among you must first be your servant,* [27] *and whoever wants to be first among you must be your slave;* [28] *just as the Son of Man did not come to be served, but to serve, and to give His life—a ransom for many."*

Power Moves and the Kingdom

4. What claims could James and John make to support their "power grab" for a prime position among the disciples?

5. What request did James and John and their mother make of Jesus?

6. Why would James and John want this position?

7. What assumption did James and John make about Jesus' kingdom?

The Servant Messiah
8. On what would Jesus base His new kingdom?

9. What would James and John have to do if they wanted to attain positions of greatness in Jesus' new kingdom?

A New Definition of Greatness
10. How did Jesus define the role of His followers?

11. Who are some examples of "great people" according to Jesus' definition?

13

12. What is the problem with the world's definition of greatness?

SMALL-GROUP
TIME:

Small-group
leaders will direct
your discussions.
Everyone will gain
more if you are
open and honest
in responding to
the questions.

Do What? (15 minutes)

Making It Personal

1. How does the mother of James and John compare to your own mother?
   - ☐ My mother would never have been so bold.
   - ☐ My mother would never have gone out of her way for me like that.
   - ☐ I can see my mother doing the exact same thing.
   - ☐ My mother wouldn't have asked—she would have demanded!
   - ☐ My mother wouldn't have encouraged such ambition.
   - ☐ Other: _____

2. Had you been one of the other disciples, what would have been your reaction to their behavior?
   - ☐ I would have been upset I hadn't thought of it first.
   - ☐ I would have understood their ambition.
   - ☐ I would have felt smug because of their failure.
   - ☐ I would have resented their attempt to "climb the ladder" at my expense.
   - ☐ I would have been sad that they let ambition threaten our fellowship.
   - ☐ Other: _____

3. What would you say is the essence of Jesus' response to the two brothers here?
   - ☐ Christians shouldn't have ambition.
   - ☐ Service, not power, is the way to get ahead.
   - ☐ Stop thinking of self and start thinking of others.
   - ☐ Christian leaders should be team-builders, not dictators.
   - ☐ Other: _____

4. When has someone's ambition (yours or someone else's) come between you and your friends?

5. In what area of your life do you need to be more of a servant? Check all that apply.
   - ☐ with family   ☐ with friends   ☐ at work
   - ☐ at school   ☐ at church   ☐ in my neighborhood

# LifePoint Review

Real greatness comes through personal sacrifice and servanthood.

"Do" Points

These "Do" points will help you begin to experience this week's "LifePoint." Be open and honest as you discuss the action points within your small group.

We have now come to the end of our last session of classes on authentic relationships. Perhaps we can summarize all of them by saying that authentic Christian relationships are modeled after how Christ relates to us. Nowhere do we see this more clearly than in today's session, where we have been called to model Jesus' servant style. This is in marked contrast to the way the world encourages us to relate to others. To better live out Jesus' servant style, here are some specific things we can do:

1. <u>Analyze how you are serving others at your church.</u> Doing so will help you see your efforts as a true calling—not something to simply keep you busy at church or to earn you brownie points with your youth pastor or church staff. It will help you consider how what you do contributes to the people you serve, instead of simply contributing to your reputation or ego.

2. <u>Get involved in one ministry through which you can serve others in a way that is truly meaningful.</u> This may be a ministry of your church; it may be an independent community service agency; it may be something you simply do on your own. What is important is that it be something that uses your talents, that truly helps people in need, and that does not focus on you and your own glory.

3. <u>Take a new look at the "servant" tasks you do, particularly in your own family.</u> Are there jobs that everyone avoids doing? Are there tasks that you only do with resentment? Take on these tasks in the spirit of Christ! Note, however, that if you are already doing all or most of these, it may be time to encourage your friends or other family members to understand the value and importance of serving each other.

13

Prayer Connection:

This is the time for developing and expressing concern for each other. Thank God for the example of servanthood He provided through the His Son. Express your thankfulness to God for those who have served you. Ask God to help you find the same kind of willingness to serve others.

Share prayer needs and requests with the group, especially those related to hearing from and responding to God. Your group facilitator will close your time in prayer.

Prayer Needs:

 now What?

Option #1

Earlier in the session, you answered the following question: In what area of your life do you need to be more of a servant? Check all that apply.

- ☐ with family _____
- ☐ with friends _____
- ☐ at work _____
- ☐ at school _____
- ☐ at church _____
- ☐ in my neighborhood _____

Review your selections. Beside each area that you checked, record one specific way you can demonstrate sacrifice and servanthood.

Option #2

You have just completed a study on authentic relationships. Hopefully, the time you have spent with your small group over the last 13 weeks has brought you closer. As a group, you may decide that you want to continue to learn and to grow together in Christ.

A covenant is a promise made to another in the presence of God. Its purpose is to indicate your intention to make yourselves available to one another for the fulfillment of the purposes you share in common. If your small group is going to continue, in a spirit of prayer, work your way through the following sentences, trying to reach an agreement on each statement pertaining to your ongoing life together. Write out your covenant like a contract, stating your purpose, goals, and the ground rules for your group.

1. The purpose of our group will be:
2. Our goals will be:
3. We will meet on _____ (day of week).
4. We will meet for _____ weeks, after which we will decide if we wish to continue as a group.
5. We will meet from _____ to _____ and we will strive to start on time and end on time.
6. We will meet at _____ (place) or we will rotate from house to house.
7. We will agree to the following ground rules for our group (check):
   - ☐ Priority: While you are in this course of study, you give the group meetings priority.
   - ☐ Participation: Everyone is encouraged to participate and no one dominates.
   - ☐ Respect: Everyone has the right to his or her own opinion, and all questions are encouraged and respected.
   - ☐ Confidentiality: Anything said in the meeting is never repeated outside the meeting.
   - ☐ Life Change: We will regularly assess our own life change goals and encourage one another in our pursuit of Christlikeness.
   - ☐ Care and Support: Permission is given to call upon each other at any time especially in times of crisis.
   - ☐ Accountability: We agree to let the members of the group hold us accountable to the commitments which each of us make in whatever loving ways we decide upon.

13

Bible Reference Notes

Use these notes to gain further understanding of the text as you study on your own.

Matthew 20:20

the mother of Zebedee's sons. In this society, women were of little worth, and thus we have this description where the mother isn't even named and where the sons are "Zebedee's" sons. In Mark's account, James and John approached Jesus directly. Regardless of the role their mother played in this incident, it is clear that they were held responsible for it (v. 24). In accordance with the general assumption about the Messiah, the disciples expected that Jesus would come into a position of authority as the new king of Israel. Those who sat on His right and His left would be His chief lieutenants. James and John were thinking in these terms in spite of the fact that Jesus had just announced His coming death (Matt. 20:17-19).

Matthew 20:22

drink the cup. This phrase means *to share the same fate.* In the Old Testament, drinking the cup is a metaphor for experiencing God's wrath. *(Examples: Ps. 75:8; Isa. 51:17-23.)* Here, the cup refers to Jesus' suffering and death for the sins of the world.

we are able. In spite of their bold assertion, they did not grasp what He meant. They probably assumed He was referring simply to being willing to share in His future, which they imagined would be one of power and prestige.

Matthew 20:24

they became indignant. As self-serving as the request of James and John had been, the response of the others was not much better. All 12 shared the view that the Kingdom would be earthly and political, with Jesus as the reigning king and them as His chief lieutenants.

Matthew 20:26

servant. Rather than becoming masters (and exercising authority), they were to become servants and meet the needs of others. The Greek word for servant, *diakonos,* from which the English word *deacon* is derived, became the most common description of church leaders in the early church.

Matthew 20:28

ransom. This is not meant to be understood in terms of a strict legal transaction in which Jesus died to somehow buy off either God or the devil, a debate that engaged theologians in times past. Instead, *ransom* was a word generally used to describe the act of freeing people from bondage, whether through the literal payment of a purchase price or through some act of deliverance.

Acknowledgments

We sincerely appreciate the great team of people who worked to develop *Authentic Relationships: Being Real in an Artificial World, Youth Edition.* Special thanks are extended to Carol Sallee for adapting the adult study for youth. We also appreciate the editorial and production team that consisted of Syble Groover, Nicole Childress, Beca Monger, and Lynn Pryor.